OSPREY
MILITARY

CAMPA

NEW ORLEANS 1815

*This print exemplifies the popular view of the Battle of New Orleans; lots of detail, none of it correct. General Pakenham on foot (he was mounted) falls back into the arms of kilted Highlanders (they were in trews) instead of his aide's, while in the background British infantry break into a full run before withering American fire. (Anne S.K. Brown Military Collection, Brown University)*

GENERAL EDITOR DAVID G. CHANDLER

**OSPREY MILITARY**

# CAMPAIGN SERIES 28

# NEW ORLEANS 1815

## ANDREW JACKSON CRUSHES THE BRITISH

### TIM PICKLES

To Ron Berlin,

Who knows the smell of powder
and apericiates the sacrifices of a soldier

best wishes

Tim Pickles

New Orleans          6 January 1995

First published in Great Britain in
1993 by OSPREY, an imprint of Reed
Consumer Books Limited, Michelin
House, 81 Fulham Road, London
SW3 6RB and Auckland, Melbourne
Singapore and Toronto.

ISBN 1-85532-360-5

Produced by DAG Publications Ltd
for Osprey Publishing Ltd.
Colour bird's eye view illustrations by
Peter Harper.
Cartography by Micromap.
*Wargaming New Orleans* by Arthur
Harman.
Wargames Consultant Duncan
Macfarlane.
Mono camerawork by M&E Repro-
ductions, North Fambridge, Essex.
Printed and bound in Hong Kong.

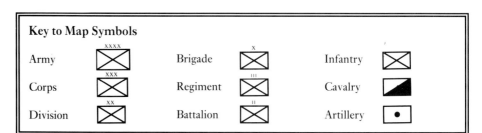

**Key to Map Symbols**

| | | | | | | |
|---|---|---|---|---|---|---|
| Army | | Brigade | | Infantry | |
| Corps | | Regiment | | Cavalry | |
| Division | | Battalion | | Artillery | |

▲ *A late 19th-century view of the battle, showing the British looking distinctly 18th-century, and the Americans dressed in 1840s uniforms or as 'Davy Crockett'. Had the British actually been able to get men-o-war up the river, as depicted, the outcome would have been different. (Courtesy of the Neal Auction Company, New Orleans)*

# CONTENTS

# The War of 1812

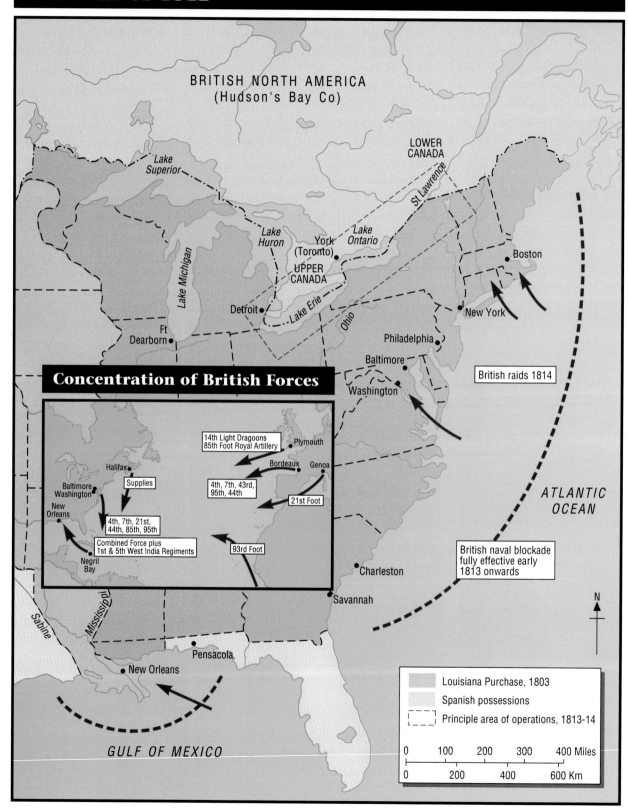

**BRITISH NORTH AMERICA**
(Hudson's Bay Co)

LOWER
CANADA

Lake
Superior

St Lawrence

Lake
Huron

York
(Toronto)

Lake
Ontario

Lake Michigan

UPPER
CANADA

Boston

Detroit

Lake Erie

Ohio

New York

Ft
Dearborn

Philadelphia

Baltimore

British raids 1814

Washington

## Concentration of British Forces

14th Light Dragoons
85th Foot Royal Artillery

Plymouth

Halifax

Bordeaux

Genoa

Supplies

4th, 7th, 43rd,
95th, 44th

Baltimore
Washington

21st Foot

New
Orleans

4th, 7th, 21st,
44th, 85th, 95th

Combined Force plus
1st & 5th West India Regiments

93rd Foot

Negril
Bay

ATLANTIC
OCEAN

Charleston

British naval blockade
fully effective early
1813 onwards

Savannah

N

Sabine

Mississippi

Pensacola

New Orleans

| | Louisiana Purchase, 1803 |
| --- | --- |
| | Spanish possessions |
| - - - | Principle area of operations, 1813-14 |

GULF OF MEXICO

| 0 | 100 | 200 | 300 | 400 Miles |
| --- | --- | --- | --- | --- |
| 0 | 200 | 400 | | 600 Km |

# ORIGINS OF THE CAMPAIGN

Whatever the War of 1812 was about, it was not about any of the oft-trumpeted causes: 'Free trade and sailors' rights', or 'The second war for American Independence'. The second of these old saws is laughable; after all, it was America that declared war, but it is amazing how these ideas persist. The author has heard a current US politician who had an ancestor involved in the New Orleans campaign declare in a speech: 'The war of 1812 started after England had defeated Napoleon. First, they conquered Canada and then used it as a base from which to attack the US. ' Needless to say, this raised an eyebrow or two amongst the Canadians present. It also seems a little strange, if one desires free trade, to declare war on the world's greatest sea power. Indeed, the disaffection of the Northern States and the formation of the Hartford Convention (a conference to discuss the secession of these states from the Union) are directly attributable to the loss of trade caused by the British blockade. As for sailors' rights, this was only an issue because English seamen jumping ship in America were being granted unquestioned immedi-ate citizenship for their useful skills. As soon as the British parliament realised that America was willing to go to war over the matter, the Orders in Council that permitted the Royal Navy to stop and search American vessels for these deserters were cancelled. Be that as it may, the war hawks in Congress, led by Henry Clay and with the tacit approval of President Madison, thought they could smell blood.

They were convinced that the taking of Canada would be 'merely a matter of marching', and, before news of the cancellation of the Orders in Council could cross the Atlantic, they declared war.

◀ *Nothing better illustrates the organization of the British Empire in 1815 than the assembly of troops for the war of 1812, which was basically a punitive raid with the aim of getting better peace terms from the Americans. The coordination of this force in a time before modern communications is mind-boggling. It is also remarkable that, within two months of the defeat of Napoleon, 10,000 troops were embarked for the Americas.*

▶ *President James Madison in younger, more vigorous days, before he became President. He inherited from President Jefferson an emasculated Army and gutted Navy; nevertheless, he allowed himself to be persuaded that declaring war on a Britain engaged in fighting Napoleon would quickly bring Canada under US domination. (Anne S.K. Brown Military Collection, Brown University)*

▲ *Major General Isaac Brock, the backbone of the Anglo-Canadian defence, who, with his indian counterpart Tecumseh, made thrusts into the US that the Americans had no answer to. His untimely death at* *the battle of Queenston Heights blunted the counterattack and gave command to Sir George Prevost, a martinet with little strategic or tactical talent. (Anne S.K. Brown Military Collection, Brown University)*

## Brother Jonathan Aroused

Initially, the American invasion met with success, principally because the Canadian colonists were caught flat-footed, but that did not last long. The Americans had gravely miscalculated in many ways. Firstly, the previous administration under President Thomas Jefferson had reduced the army and navy to an almost ridiculously small force, necessitating the use of state militias in offensive as well as defensive operations. Secondly, many of the settlers just over the border were American loyalists who, just

over 30 years before, had left the United States in order to remain subjects of the Crown. Thirdly, the Generals chosen to lead the troops against the settlers had only one qualification: they had fought in the Revolution. The biggest mistake, though, was assuming that the French Canadians would welcome American troops as liberators. The French might not have liked British rule, but they viewed rule from Washington with horror. The US also seems to have completely forgotten about the Indians who, even within the US, were well disposed to the British.

The initial American success consisted mainly of overwhelming forces pushing aside unprepared garrison troops and then burning to the ground York, the capital of Upper Canada. These successes were brought to an end when the army was taunted into taking on a force of Canadian militia, Indians, and two British line regiments (the 49th and 89th) in a European open-field-type action at Chrysler's Farm. Although the Anglo-Canadians were outnumbered three to one, they sent their foes scurrying back across the St Lawrence. Canada was never again seriously threatened. American disasters continued, particularly with the Anglo-Canadians under Major General Isaac Brock and the Indians under the great Shawnee chief Tecumseh. Even when these two leaders fell in battle (Brock at Queenston heights and Tecumseh at the Battle of the Thames), the only result was the blunting of the thrust into the States. Canada was safe.

## Veterans to America

The rest of the campaign consisted mainly of raids on the coast by the Royal Navy until the defeat, abdication and exile of the Emperor Napoleon in 1814. Troops fresh from their success in the Peninsular war were transported to America, and a punitive campaign began in earnest. The first major engagement of 1814 was at Bladensburg, outside Washington. British troops had landed and raided the coast, and then their commander, Major General Robert Ross, with the enthusiastic encouragement of Rear Admiral Cockburn and Captain George de Lacy Evans, his Deputy Assistant Adjutant General, decided to strike at the Capital. The US army that met him on the field of

▲ *The burning of Wash-ington. In this contempo-rary print, Rear Admiral Cockburn (extreme left) confers with General Ross as British troops move through the city with fire-brands looking for the public buildings. (Courtesy of Historical Military Productions, New Orleans)*

▶ *Admiral Sir George Cockburn, who raided the*

*American coastal towns riding a white horse and leading a company of sailors. He also led the party that burnt the pub-lic buildings of Washing-ton in reprisal for the burning of York, Upper Canada. He and George de Lacy Evans were great believers in pressing home the attack with the bayo-net. (Anne S. K. Brown Military Collection, Brown University)*

Bladensburg, in addition to its field commander, also had the Secretary of War and the President (the nominal Commander-in-Chief) with it. The ensu-ing discussions as to who was actually in charge were brought to an end when, with a few volleys and a bayonet charge by the British, it all became aca-demic. With the exception of a marine detachment, the American army broke and fled. The marines covered the retreat as best they could and then with-drew. As the British entered the American capital, the staff were fired upon from a private house and General Ross's horse was killed. By the time troops reached the house it was empty, and in reprisal the house was burnt. This was the only private property intentionally burnt by the occupying troops but, in reprisal for the burning of York, the public buildings were all put to the torch. The White House survived until the British officers had partaken of the meal prepared for President Madison, which he had abandoned in his haste. After partaking of a Port Wine that Rear Admiral Cockburn described as 'super excellent', the incendiaries were set and the house gutted. Today the house is painted white to cover the scorch marks. As British troops entered the city the commander of the US Navy yard set fire to the installation to deny its supplies to the enemy. This blaze, fed by tar and cordage, spread to parts of the city and did considerable damage. Their job complete, the British army re-embarked and sailed for Baltimore.

General Ross and his troops landed and approached Baltimore's outer defences by land while Admiral Cochrane sent in ships to bombard the city's main defence work, Fort McHenry, from the harbour approaches. Again, Admiral Cockburn and Captain de Lacy Evans urged General Ross on to a quick victory. When the two armies met at North Point, the outer defence position, there was something more of a fight than at Bladensburg. However, British troops turned the American flank and the Americans retreated to the defences of Fort McHenry. Unfortunately, during the action General Ross was killed by a stray bullet while heading back from the advance guard to bring up the main force. The command devolved by seniority on the colonel of the 44th, who advanced towards the fort but, on seeing the scale of the defences, decided not to press the attack. Under cover of the naval bombardment, the army re-embarked the fleet then upped anchor and sailed over the horizon.

▼ *The Battle of North Point, from a contemporary American print. The British advance towards the American* *position while light troops work around the American left. (Historical Military Productions, New Orleans)*

# PLANS AND PREPARATIONS

The Americans could not be sure where the British would strike next, but they could make a very good guess that it would be the city controlling the Mississippi River – perhaps the richest city on the continent – New Orleans. In January 1814 the Horse Guards received a report they had commissioned on the feasibility of taking New Orleans; it was comprehensive and accurate. The climate in summer was found to be very unhealthy, with humidity and temperatures that were all but deadly to Europeans, and with an abundance of mosquitoes and yellow fever rampant (though the connection between the two had not yet been discovered). Summer and autumn were also the hurricane seasons. Any amphibious operation, as this would be, would be impossible before early December.

On 25 November 1814 Admiral Cochrane arrived in Negril Bay, Jamaica, with his flagship the *Tonnant*, and began assembling the fleet which would carry the expedition to attack and capture the city. The troops of the American expedition were to be augmented by fresh ones from Europe and beyond, and he was taking two Black regiments from Jamaica, to act as a garrison for the conquered city during the summer months, when the climate would kill white troops.

## The Honour of Command

In London discussions were continuing as to who General Ross's replacement should be. Wellington refused the command before it was really offered to him; Lord Hill was considered, as was Sir Thomas Picton. Finally, the honour went to Major General Sir Edward Pakenham, KB. With him as second-in-command went Major General Samuel Gibbs.

In Jamaica, Major General Keane, who arrived with reinforcements only to find himself commanding the expedition, was still trying to organise what troops he had. Major General John Lambert had been sent out to take command until Pakenham's arrival, but delays in his transport led to his arriving after the new commander.

As Pakenham and Gibbs continued on their way to Jamaica, the secret orders revealing the objective of the expedition were opened. If there was any surprise, it was because the London newspapers had so accurately guessed at them, and published them, well before the troops' departure. When the new C-in-C arrived at Negril Bay, he found that he had missed Admiral Cochrane by hours. As quickly as possible he sailed to join his command.

The army of the United States was beginning to emerge from under the dead wood of the 'revolutionary' high command. Incompetent bungling at the beginning of the campaign had forced the advancement of new general officers such as Harrison and Winfield Scott, who had been able to meet British regulars with some degree of success. The threat to the south brought forth perhaps the best of the lot, and, indeed, the only logical choice, Major General Andrew Jackson.

In a way, Jackson's problem was the same as that of Hitler in the Second World War. He knew an attack was coming, he knew its objective, but he did not know when or from where it would come. On balance he thought it probable that the enemy would land on the gulf coast, perhaps at Mobile or Pensacola, and then march towards Baton Rouge, coinciding with a naval blockade, thus cutting off New Orleans by both land and sea. In fact there were already some British troops in Pensacola, and Jackson decided to deal with these first.

## British Allies

Within the Spanish territories of Florida the officially neutral officials were, in fact, well disposed to the British, who had just thrown the French out of Spain and re-established the legitimate monarchy.

The American Government's view of all this was that the British attack would begin from Mobile, that Spain was likely to send troops from Mexico to support them, and that, while all this was going on, a slave revolt in New Orleans would paralyse the local troops. Strangely enough, although this idea was first voiced in September, it was not until November that any military stores were sent south. It is not unreasonable to suppose that someone, somewhere wanted Jackson to fail.

As early as April 1814, Captain Pigot, RN, had been sent to raise the Creek Indians to the British cause. His report on their enthusiasm seems to have been one of the factors in the decision to put the plan of capturing New Orleans into operation. On reading this report Admiral Cochrane, on his own initiative, had landed Major Edward Nichols, RM, and 100 men with orders to organize the Indians. He had with him a supply of obsolete Foot Guard coats and cocked hats, which would give them a rudimentary uniform, and muskets with which to arm them.

Jackson sent an aide to Governor Don Mateo Mariniqe, demanding an explanation of British operations on Spanish territory. Don Mateo replied that Jackson was impertinent, and that the Indians were entitled to protection. The British build-up in Pensacola continued.

## American Reaction

In anticipation of British operations in Mobile, Jackson sent a reinforcement of 160 men to help with the defence of Fort Bowyer, which guarded its harbour. His plans were helped by the Royal Navy going on another mission first, a visit to the last of the old-style pirates, Jean Lafitte.

Officially, Jackson was ordered not to attack Spanish territory; unofficially, he was encouraged to do so, albeit on his own authority. The American attack on Pensacola met with virtually no Spanish opposition. The defence crumbled so quickly that the British only just managed to evacuate the city.

The attack on Fort Bowyer, when it finally did occur, was decided by luck. As the Royal Marines and indians were being held in check by artillery from the fort's defences, ships of the Royal Navy dropped anchor off Mobile Point to set up a bom-

▲ *Jean Lafitte, as popular history and Hollywood would have him, the patriot-pirate and an American version of Robin Hood, who happily gave up gallant piratical ways to serve his country. (Courtesy of the Louisiana State Museum)*

bardment. As the attack developed, a lucky American shot cut the cable of HMS *Hermes*, and the vessel drifted towards the fort. After being well raked by the fort's guns, she ran aground and was burnt by her captain to prevent her capture.

One remark in the final defiant reply of the Spanish Governor of Pensacola, before Jackson's successful attack, had stung the general. Among his other accusations, the Governor accused the US of harbouring pirates. As he rode back towards New Orleans, Jackson determined to do away with these 'hellish banditti'. The influence of the pirates of Barataria was far more pervasive in the city than he realised, and some of the most respected citizens had a cosy working relationship with the Lafittes.

## A Pirate King

Jean Lafitte and his brothers were French creoles from San Domingo who were displaced when the British captured the island. On reaching New Orleans they found themselves to be round pegs in round holes. Jean became the front man and organizer of the rather disorganized pirate band he found in the district just below the city, called Barataria. His easy charm and unscrupulous character made him the perfect conduit between the ruffianly pirates and haughty but corruptible creoles.

When a way of life is past, no matter how degenerate it might have been, the public imagination seems to endow it with a glamour that would amaze those who had to endure it. When apologists for Lafitte's band talk of them taking ships and treasure as if they were a latter-day Robin Hood and his merry men, they never mention prisoners. This is for the simple piratical reason that 'dead men tell no tales'. Lafitte operated under letters of marque from Cartagena, a city held by Mexican revolutionaries with whom he had a flourishing arms trade. This was extremely embarrassing for the US Government. Lafitte was also a slave trader, with the added refinement that he did not trouble to collect them from a friendly African chief and sail across the Atlantic with them; he merely waited until the unarmed vessels came within his reach and took them.

Lafitte's lawyer was Edward Livingston, the black sheep of a very prominent family in New York

▲ *Edward Livingston, brilliant but corrupt, was forced to go south by factions who would put up with him no longer. His journey was eased, and* *possibly his introduction to Jean Lafitte effected, by his masonic connections. (Courtesy of the Louisiana State Museum)*

State, whose chequered career had given him ample opportunity to display both his brilliance and his corruption. One of his congressional colleagues, John Randolph of Roanoke, Virginia, said of him: 'He is brilliant but utterly corrupt, he stinks and shines like rotten mackerel by moonlight'. The fact that this taunt did not result in a challenge to a duel is very telling.

One thing the Lafittes and their confederates could not be accused of was stupidity, and they realised that they had outlived their time. The only question was how to survive. The turning point had been the sale of the Louisiana territory to the US Government by Napoleon.

With the arrival of a federal official, William Charles Cole Claiborne, first as territorial and lately as state governor, their situation had changed for

# Theatre of Campaign

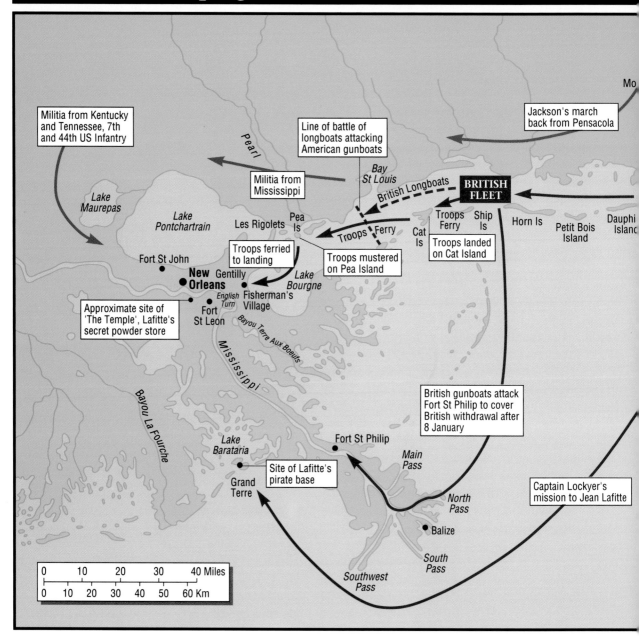

Militia from Kentucky and Tennessee, 7th and 44th US Infantry

Line of battle of longboats attacking American gunboats

Jackson's march back from Pensacola

Militia from Mississippi

Bay St Louis

British Longboats

BRITISH FLEET

Lake Maurepas

Lake Pontchartrain

Les Rigolets

Pearl

Pea Is

Troops Ferry

Cat Is

Troops Ferry

Ship Is

Horn Is

Petit Bois Island

Dauphi Island

Fort St John

Troops ferried to landing

New Orleans

Gentilly

Lake Bourgne

Troops mustered on Pea Island

Troops landed on Cat Island

Approximate site of 'The Temple', Lafitte's secret powder store

English Turn

Fisherman's Village

Fort St Leon

Bayou Terre Aux Boeufs

Mississippi

Bayou La Fourche

Lake Barataria

Grand Terre

Site of Lafitte's pirate base

Fort St Philip

Main Pass

British gunboats attack Fort St Philip to cover British withdrawal after 8 January

North Pass

Captain Lockyer's mission to Jean Lafitte

Balize

South Pass

Southwest Pass

Mo

| 0 | 10 | 20 | 30 | 40 Miles |
| 0 | 10 | 20 | 30 | 40 | 50 | 60 Km |

ever. From the time of his first appointment in 1803, Claiborne had an uphill struggle. Contemptuously referred to as 'Calybo' by the creoles, he dutifully steered the territory towards statehood, law, and order. When statehood finally came, in 1812, it was no more than just that he became the first governor. After that a mini-war between the pirates and customs men broke out. Captured

pirates had no difficulty in raising bail and then jumping it, but this action made them criminals in law, not just in fact (as they had been all along).

The final straw came in 1813. On 24 November Claiborne offered a $500 reward for Lafitte, who three days later issued his own proclamation offering $5,000 for the governor! Lafitte had made his first mistake; in declaring war on the governor he

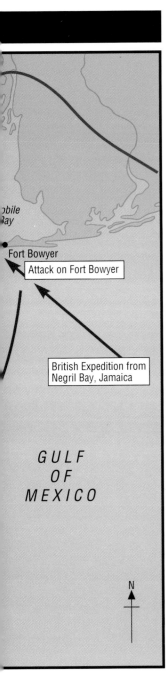

Fort Bowyer

Attack on Fort Bowyer

British Expedition from Negril Bay, Jamaica

GULF
OF
MEXICO

N

◀ *As soon as Admiral Cochrane entered the Gulf of Mexico with the invasion fleet, he and Andrew Jackson began a game of chess in which neither player could see all the pieces. The first move on Pensacola was checked by Jackson capturing the city against his stated orders. However, by taking Jackson's 'pawns', the gunboats in Lake Bourgne, Cochrane made sure that the next British move, whatever it might be, would be a surprise.*

At about this time Commodore Daniel T. Patterson arrived in the USS *Carolina* to clean out the nest of vipers once and for all. In this darkest hour for Lafitte, like an answer to a prayer, Captain Nicholas Lockyer RN, accompanied by Major Nichols RM, turned up at the pirate headquarters in Barataria with an offer.

England would not stand for piracy, but, if Lafitte would assist the British in taking New Orleans and put his ships under Royal Navy orders, he would be rewarded; he and his captains would be given rank in the Royal Navy. Never for a moment did Lafitte seriously consider the offer. If the British won and stayed, he would be under the orders of the world's greatest sea power, which would have no compunction in blowing him out of the water if he tried to return to his old ways. If the Americans won, he would never again be able to use Barataria bay as a safe harbour. Now, though, he had something with which to bargain. Asking the British for two weeks to consider the offer, he immediately wrote to Governor Claiborne, informing him of the meeting and pledging his loyalty to the United States. He also informed the governor of the price for that loyalty - a free pardon for himself and his brothers.

### Crime and Punishment

Claiborne was in a difficult situation. His friend Andrew Jackson had already been writing to him on the prospects of the British attacking, advising speedy preparations. The previous military commander of the area, General James Wilkinson, had managed to divert most of the cash intended for the upkeep of the fortifications into his own pocket, and the population was not exactly flocking to the colours.

Claiborne was desperate to get any local volunteers he could, so, supported by General Jaques Villeré of the militia, he wrote to Jackson, recommending acceptance of Lafitte's offer. However, with Jackson away dealing with the threat in Pensacola, there was no way that Commodore Patterson could be prevented from carrying out his appointed mission of destroying the pirates' headquarters.

When the attack was carried out there was no resistance, as Lafitte had ordered. The landing party

had declared war on the nation. In January 1814 the pirates attacked a group of revenue officers, killing or wounding them all. In July a Federal Grand Jury finally indicted the Lafittes for piracy. Only a few days later Pierre Lafitte was captured in the city, jailed without bond, and clapped in irons. Despite Edward Livingston's best efforts, there he remained.

◄ *Pirates in their (murky) lair: (left to right) Renato Beluche, Jean Lafitte, Pierre Lafitte and Dominique You. Here we see the pirates for what they were, scheming murderers, with gold as their one god. Human life was to be valued only if it could bring them a profit. They were, truly, Jackson's 'Hellish Banditi'. (Courtesy of the Louisiana State Museum)*

▶ *Near right: William Charles Cole Claiborne. A long-time friend of Jackson, he nevertheless thought that, as Governor, he should have de facto command of all the troops in the area, and clashed with Jackson over this. When Jackson was quite sure that the British would not come that way, he put him in command of*

*the troops on the plain of Gentilly. (Courtesy of the Louisiana State Museum)*

▶ *Far right: Commodore Daniel Patterson, USN.*

*Sent down to clean out the pirates, he ended up being forced to organize the west bank shore batteries when all but one of his little flotilla was captured by the British.*

◀ *Far left: The signing of the Louisiana Purchase. This early 20th century magazine illustration shows everything that someone celebrating the 100th anniversary would want to see, including a portrait of Louis XIV, after whom the colony was named. However, this does not change the fact that, in selling the colony to America, Napoleon had broken the terms of the treaty of San Ildefonso by which the colony had been returned to France, thus making America's legal right to their new possession tenuous at best. (Private Collection)*

◀ *Left: The transfer of the Louisiana Territory in 1803. The ceremony took place in the Place d'Armes, New Orleans, the city parade ground. To observe the technical niceties of the transfer of the colony from Spain to France to America, first the Spanish flag was flown, then the tricolour, which was taken down to be replaced by the stars and stripes. However, this legal fiction did not change the fact that, under international law, the colony should have been returned to Spain. (Anne S.K. Brown Military Collection, Brown University)*

found caches of guns and ammunition (though only a fraction of what Lafitte actually had), captured 80 prisoners and took several chests of treasure, one of which was later to prove Lafitte's undoing. Whether by accident or by Lafitte's design, they also found letters from some prominent citizens of New Orleans, linking them with piratical activities and thus ensuring that he could not be prosecuted without a very large can of worms being opened.

By the time Jackson arrived back in the city, the situation seemed, if anything, worse than before. Only 1,000 regulars and 2,000 militia had been assembled. General Villeré and Edward Livingston had been deputed by the legislature to urge Jackson to accept Lafitte's offer. Jackson refused and made a counter-proposal – that the legislature should suspend the writ of *habeas corpus* in order to allow him to press seamen forcibly into service, particularly for the converted sloop *Louisiana*, which had no crew at all.

▲ *Major General Jaques Villeré, commander of the Louisiana State Militia. He was off raising his troops from the coast when the British captured both his home and his son. He returned to find his son, who had escaped* *from the British, under arrest on Jackson's orders for dereliction of duty. The year after the battle he succeeded Claiborne as Governor of Louisiana. (Courtesy of the Louisiana State Museum)*

▲ *Lieutenant Thomas ap Catesby Jones, Jackson's 'eyes' on Lake Bourgne, who was captured along with his little flotilla by* *Captain Lockyer and his gunboats.*

This seems almost fantastic. America had declared war on the pretext of preventing the impressment of its sailors by the British. Now one of its own generals was proposing precisely the same course of action. To the legislature this smacked of the sort of thing they had had to put up with under General Wilkinson, and they would not even consider the idea. One of the main reasons that seamen were in short supply was that, unlike the army, the navy paid no bounty to join. In an attempt to correct this the legislature voted $6,000 to Commodore Patterson to use for bounties.

Patterson's little fleet consisted of six gunboats and the unmanned *Louisiana*. One gunboat was sent

to Fort St Philip on the Mississippi to give warning if the British fleet were to try beating up river. (This was highly unlikely, as no ship of the line could get over the sand bars at the river's mouth. ) The other five were sent to patrol Lake Bourgne under the command of Lieutenant Thomas ap Catesby Jones. Lake Bourgne was also protected by sand bars and shallows; no problem for the gunboats, which drew only five feet, but impassable for a ship of the line.

Thus, with his 'eyes' on the main approaches and with more troops arriving or expected daily, Jackson was beginning to feel a little more secure.

### The Battle of Lake Bourgne

The knowledge of US troop movements that Admiral Cochrane had obtained indicated that the

# The Battle of Lake Bourgne

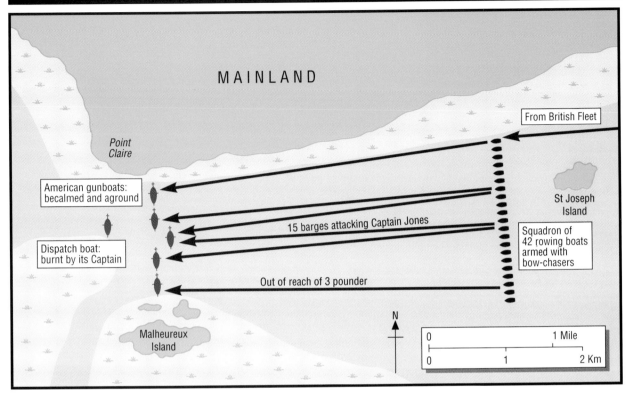

main American force was poised to resist a British landing at Mobile. He therefore expected to effect complete surprise when he arrived with his fleet off Lake Bourgne on 13 December.

He was disappointed when the first thing he saw was Catesby Jones's gunboats obviously heading back to their base to give news of the British arrival. As British vessels attempted to give chase, they ran into the sand bars and stuck. What the Royal Navy did not realise was that the Americans themselves had been stuck only hours before. A freak combination of low tides and offshore winds had made Lake Bourgne shallower than usual. Only the incoming tide had allowed them to sail off, but as soon as the tide stopped running, at about 0100, they stuck fast again.

Admiral Cochrane began to make plans. The next morning saw 42 British longboats carrying 1,200 sailors and Royal Marines, each boat mounting a carronade in the bows, steadily pulling towards the gunboats. Before the British flotilla came within range of the American guns, its commander, Captain Lockyer (he of the visit to Jean Lafitte),

▲ *As the American gunboats run to tell Jackson of the arrival of the British fleet, they are grounded between Point Claire and Malheureux Island and are approached by a British attack squadron of armed rowing boats manned by sailors and marines. The small bow-chasers on the boats were only effective at close range, and while it is true that the Americans were outnumbered, the battle was an example of Royal Navy improvisation and bravery at its best. As the rowing boats closed with the Americans the Royal Marine boarding parties conducted a short but furious hand-to-hand fight and the vessels were taken.*

ordered a halt so that the attacking force could eat dinner. Thus fortified, they pressed home the attack.

Many American writers have made much of the number of men and boats in the British flotilla, but it is nonetheless remarkable that a force of rowing boats could attack and take five gunboats formed in line of battle. At 1230, when the fighting ended, the victorious British losses were seventeen killed and 77 wounded; the Americans lost ten killed, 35 wounded and 86 captured. The wounded included

▲ *The Battle of Lake Bourgne. The grounded US vessels wait for the onslaught of the British rowing boats as they press on through the* *Americans' broadsides. (Courtesy of The Historic New Orleans Collection, Museum Research Center)*

both Lieutenant Catesby Jones and Captain Lockyer. In addition to the gunboats, a supply ship that had been cut off was blown up by her captain to prevent the British capturing her.

Admiral Cochrane was now free to operate as he wished. Indeed, apart from the obvious fact that the British had arrived, Jackson never found out what the fleet was doing or where the army would land.

## Disembarkation

As the whole landing was going to have to be carried out using longboats, owing to the shallowness of the lake, it was necessary to get the army as close to the coast as possible. The decision was made to assemble the troops on Pea Island, and they were duly ferried

there. Unfortunately the island was completely barren, so all supplies had to be ferried in as well. Moreover, the weather was unseasonably cold even for December, and many of the negro troops of the 1st and 5th West India regiments died from the cold.

Cochrane had another piece of luck when he was approached by some Spanish fishermen whose village was near the mouth of one of the bayous emptying into the lake. They had little love for the 'Americans' who had come since 1803, and were aware of the friendly relations between England and Spain. They told the Admiral of a canal, which was difficult to find but which they would show him, leading right to the banks of the Mississippi and the road to New Orleans.

Things were looking bad for Andrew Jackson. His entire naval force was now reduced to the gunboat *Carolina* and the sloop *Louisiana*. Furthermore, he could not get any reliable local maps of the area on which to work out the routes the British might possibly take to effect their landing. This was because of the active, or tacit, involvement of the outlying community in smuggling. No one wanted their own private access to the Gulf of Mexico known to the Federal Government. However, Jackson had tried to cover this by ordering all private waterways blocked, specifically to deny their use to the British.

## Strange Bedfellows

Once again Jackson was approached on the Lafitte question, this time by Bernard de Marigny, a member of the State Legislature, at the head of a committee of creole gentlemen. Once more the suggestion was rejected.

In desperation the committee turned to Judge Dominick Hall, before whom any cases against the pirates, and their newly discovered local confederates, would be heard. Judge Hall had no wish to proceed with a potentially embarrassing case, and suggested that the legislature resolve to suspend the proceedings against the pirates if the pirates would fight for the United States against the British.

The legislature immediately passed the act, and Governor Claiborne issued a proclamation to that effect. Judge Hall immediately released all the pirates and sent a pass to Jean Lafitte (who was in hiding), allowing him to come into the city with impunity.

Lafitte was at his lowest ebb but poised for his hour of glory. His two lawyers, Livingston and John Grimes, both of whom had been handsomely paid before Patterson's raid, had already prepared a suit against the United States Government for the return of his 'personal property'. Lafitte was almost completely without ready cash, but now was not the time to press the suit. If the British won he would probably be hanged, but if the Americans won, and if he could contrive a key role for himself and his men in that victory, an admiralty court would probably be well disposed to returning his treasure.

Finally, on 18 December, Jackson's engineer officer, Arsene Lacarriere Latour, who unbeknown to Jackson was a close friend of Lafitte and Livingston, convinced the General that it was in his interests to at least hear the pirate out. No record of what was discussed at the meeting was kept, but it is not hard to guess at the proceedings.

With his considerable charm Lafitte once more offered the services of his men and then played his trump card. In his capacity as an arms dealer to the Mexicans he had, at a secret location called the Temple, vast stocks of powder, ball and shot. In spite of everything he had said before, and in spite of his personal dislike of the pirates, Jackson accepted. After that, whatever else his forces might have been short of, they were not short of ammunition.

The Baratarians were organised in three companies and sent to reinforce the forts guarding the main approaches to the city: Petit Coquilles, St Philip, and St John. Jean Lafitte himself took Major Michael Reynolds to his secret ammunition store. The only pirates actually to take part in the action were two gun crews, one under Lafitte's elder brother, who called himself Dominique You, and the other under his 'oncle', Renato Beluche. Lafitte's location during the action is a matter of speculation, but it is fairly safe to say that he was not near any of the fighting.

▲ *Andrew Jackson: a print of a painting said to have been executed during his organization of the defence of New Orleans. His initial popularity with the citizens started* *to wane when they began to suspect (rightly) that this defence could include burning the city. (Marquis James,* **Life of Andrew Jackson***)*

# THE OPPOSING COMMANDERS

## The British

Major General Sir Edward Michael Pakenham, KB, was born in Ireland in 1778, the sixth child and second son of Lord Longford. Although his father was a Royal Navy captain, Edward did not go to sea, but was gazetted as a lieutenant in the 92nd Foot (Gordon Highlanders) at the age of 16. Over the next three years he purchased his captaincy in the Gordons and transferred to the 23rd Light Dragoons to obtain his Majority.

In 1798 a French invasion force under General Jean Marie Humbert landed in Ireland and Pakenham's regiment was one of those opposing it. The invasion, of course, failed, but at the battle of Ballinamuck General Gerard Lake particularly noted Pakenham's distinguished service, and as a result he was given the Lieutenant Colonelcy of the 64th Foot.

In 1801 he and his regiment were sent to the West Indies to take part in operations against the Danish and Swedish islands. While on that side of the Atlantic he spent some time in Halifax, Nova Scotia, where the Governor Sir George Prevost opined that the 'hatred of Jefferson against England' might 'mislead the ignorant and unprincipled populations of the great southern towns'.

When war with France resumed in 1803, his regiment was sent to join in the invasion of the French colony of St Lucia. There he received a neck wound, which gave him a slight tilt of the head, and he was invalided home.

In 1805 he obtained a brevet Colonelcy and was given command of the 7th Foot (Royal Fusiliers). In 1806 he attended the wedding of his sister Kitty and Major General Sir Arthur Wellesley, KB. In 1807 he and his regiment were with Wellesley at Copenhagen, where he took part in another amphibious landing.

1808 saw the 7th ordered out to the West Indies. On 1 February 1809 he was wounded in the neck

▶ *Major General Sir Edward Michael Pakenham, KB. In this print of the only complete portrait of him, Pakenham stands before a rendition of the battle of Salamanca. His uniform is that of Wellington's Adjutant General, with its embroidery in threes identical to that of a lieutenant general, but in silver rather than gold. This, and the aguilette rather than the regulation pair of epaulettes, has led some to mistake his rank. In addition to the Order of the Bath, he also wears the Army Gold Cross with four bars and the Portuguese Order of the Tower and Sword. (Alcee Fortier, A History of Louisiana)*

▲ *Vice Admiral Alexander Cochrane. This print, after the portrait by William Beechy, shows the courtly intelligent commander of contemporary British accounts. However, Wellington himself implied in a letter that it was Cochrane's desire for prize money that led the British to disaster at New Orleans, though his plan of taking the West Bank batteries almost brought victory. (Historical Military Productions, New Orleans)*

again, while leading his regiment during the successful attack on Martinique. By a quirk of fate, this wound corrected his head tilt. Later that same year he was appointed Adjutant General to Marquis Wellington in the Peninsula. He was an excellent staff officer but he still disliked 'this damned clerking business'.

In August 1810, Pakenham finally got a brigade consisting of his own 7th Foot and the 76th (Cameron Highlanders), which he commanded at Busaco and Fuentes d'Onoro. In 1811 he was promoted Major General. At Salamanca in 1812 his brigade was the key to Wellington's victory, which led his brother-in-law to say of him: 'Pakenham may not be the brightest genius, but my partiality for him does not lead me astray when I tell you that he

is one of the best we have.' Pakenham might have disliked staff work, but Wellington had great regard for him in this capacity and deplored his absence from Waterloo.

During the invasion of France in 1813, Pakenham commanded a Division and was subsequently made a Knight of the Bath. On 24 October 1814 he was given command of the land forces of the American Expedition. He was given instructions not to halt operations until he received news from a special emissary from the Prince Regent that peace had been signed. He was not to believe any rumours.

It has been said that he was never to learn of his final elevation to Knight Grand Cross of the Bath as the despatch only arrived after his death at New Orleans. However, this was not a promotion. The Order had been reorganised in 1814 from a single class to one with three classes; the despatch merely confirmed his position as a knight of the highest rank.

Vice Admiral Sir Alexander Forester Inglis Cochrane was born in 1758, the youngest son of the Earl of Dundonald. As a younger son he had the usual career choices of the church or the military. He chose the navy and became a lieutenant (a rank then obtainable by purchase) in 1778.

In 1780 he was wounded in an action off Martinique. During the American War he served on the North American Station under Admiral Rodney. A good friend of his was killed at Yorktown, and as a result he did not have much time for Americans.

After the treaty of Paris he was on half pay until 1790, when he was given a frigate which he operated as a commerce raider against the French with considerable success. During the Egyptian campaign of 1798-1801 he commanded HMS *Ajax* and superintended troop landings, thereafter acting as close support for the army by organising a flotilla of small boats to maintain contact between them and the fleet.

Cochrane's skill at amphibious landings did not go unnoticed. During the peace of Amiens he was again on half pay, but on the resumption of hostilities he was returned to duty and promoted Rear Admiral. With his flagship, the 74-gun HMS *Northumberland*, four other ships of the line and three frigates, he was sent to chase a French squadron that eventually led him to the West Indies.

▲ *Above: Lieutenant Colonel Alexander Dickson, RA, depicted in an engraving of c.1816 wearing, amongst other decorations, the Portuguese Order of the Tower and Sword and the Army Gold Cross. (Private Collection)*

▲ *Above right: Major General Keane. Though something of a 'pampered pet' in his early career, he served well at New Orleans and certainly did better than some of his contemporaries expected of him. During the attack his advance guard was an independent command*

*under Rennie, and the 93rd were marched off to reinforce Gibbs, so his command was reduced to the 1st West India Regiment and a detachment of Rifles. (Author's Collection)*

▶ *Opposite page: Major General John Lambert, whose main order to support whichever attack broke the American line became redundant when the whole British attack fell apart. He succeeded to the command of the expeditionary force by the fact that he was the only general officer on his feet by the end of the battle.*

The French got away, but while in the islands Cochrane met Nelson and continued to serve under him, gaining fame for himself in the action at San Domingo on 6 February 1806. He also commanded the amphibious landing on the island of Martinique, where Lieutenant Colonel Edward Pakenham was wounded. For this action he was created a Knight of the Bath.

When Nelson was ordered home, he appointed Cochrane Commander-in-Chief of the Leeward Islands, a command he exercised from the deck of his ship rather than from a shore-bound office. In 1809 he was promoted Vice Admiral, and the following year he commanded the successful assault on Guadeloupe, the last French possession in the West Indies.

He was still serving as governor of that island when he was informed of his appointment to command the North American Station. He spent the

When Dickson arrived in the Peninsula, still only a captain, Wellington was so impressed with him that he engineered his appointment as commander of the Portuguese artillery so that he could use him in senior positions. By 1813 Wellington had formally appointed him chief of all the Allied artillery in the Peninsula, where he was universally acknowledged as the finest gunner of his time. Although he was still only a captain, his skill made him a perfectly acceptable commander to officers who outranked him in the British service.

Major General John Keane was a product of privilege and patronage in the British Army. He was a captain at 13, and a series of home-service appointments saw him a Colonel in 1809, when he saw his first action under Wellington in the Peninsula.

Although his service did not bring him any particular distinction, in 1814 he was promoted to Major General and put in charge of the reinforcements being sent to General Ross in America. Ross's death meant that he arrived to find himself *de facto* commander of the expedition.

As soon as this was known in England, Major General John Lambert was sent to replace Keane. In order not to offend Keane's influential friends, Lambert was sent out with reinforcements. It just so happened that, because of Lambert's seniority, he would then be in command. He was sent with specific orders on how the landing was to be effected.

Major General Samuel Gibbs, a veteran of India and the amphibious attack on Java, was to be Pakenham's immediate second in command. He was a very competent officer and was travelling out in the same ship as Pakenham. Unfortunately, the delayed arrival of Pakenham, Gibbs, and Lambert left Keane, whose place in the command structure was still to be decided, in command of the landing after all. The bad luck of the campaign had another manifestation.

Colonel John Fox Burgoyne, the engineer officer, was the illegitimate son of the General who lost the battle of Saratoga during the American Revolution. The engineer equivalent of Dickson, he was quite brilliant, as could be seen in his construction of the lines of Torres Vedras for Wellington. However, a simple dam he constructed at New Orleans collapsed.

winter in England planning the campaign. On 1 April 1814 he arrived at Bermuda in his flagship, the 80-gun HMS *Tonnant*, to relieve his predecessor, Sir John Borlase Warren. During the American campaign of 1814 he had command of all the naval operations in the Chesapeake and the bombardment of Baltimore. Sailing away from Bermuda, he took his fleet to Negril Bay, Jamaica, and began to prepare for the attack on New Orleans.

Colonel Alexander Dickson was born in 1777 and entered the Royal Artillery after attending the Royal Military Academy at Woolwich. From entering the service in 1794 he was constantly employed, and his genius was evident from the start. He was sent to the Americas with the ill-fated South American expedition, and was at Buenos Aires with Harry Smith, the young rifles officer who was to serve with him at New Orleans and become famous in his own right.

## The Americans

Major General Andrew Jackson was the third child of Andrew Jackson of Carrickfergus, Ireland, who had emigrated to the Carolinas in 1765. He was born in 1767, about a month after his father's death. His mother, obviously a woman of great courage, was alone for her confinement, and had a great influence on little Andrew. The brightest of the Jackson siblings, he used a musket from the time he could carry one and was a reckless horseman. He was a tall, gangly, somewhat frail youth, but would fight at the drop of a hat.

During the Revolutionary War the Jacksons joined the rebels, the elder brother, Hugh, being killed at the battle of Stono Ferry in 1779. The next year 13-year-old Andrew and his 16-year-old brother Robert joined Colonel William R. Davies' Regiment of Dragoons, who were operating against Colonel Banastre Tarleton. In April 1781 Andrew and Robert were captured while out foraging.

According to the story, that same day Andrew was ordered to clean the boots of a British officer and, when he refused, the officer struck him on the head with his sword, leaving him with a permanent scar and a permanent hatred of the British. The story may be apocryphal, as both brothers were

reported wounded, but whether Andrew's wound was obtained during his capture or from an arrogant officer, the scar and resentment were real.

The Jackson brothers caught smallpox and were eventually released to their mother for treatment. The brothers were saved but, unfortunately, while their mother was treating other victims of the epidemic in Charles Town, she caught the disease and died. Her grave was never found.

In 1787 Andrew passed the American bar and became a travelling lawyer, settling in Nashville. In 1796 he was a member of the Convention that framed the constitution for Tennessee in becoming the 16th State. In 1797 he was appointed the State's first congressman, and the next year he was elected senator. In the same year he decided he did not like living in Washington and resigned his seat to take up the post of justice of the Tennessee supreme court, which he retained for the next six years.

However, his legal duties did not prevent him from becoming a skilled and enthusiastic duellist. In 1801 Jackson was elected Commanding General of the Tennessee Militia, a duty which he tackled enthusiastically. Unlike many militia generals, he was good at it.

While in Washington he met and formed a close friendship with William C. C. Claiborne, so his dis-

◀ *'The Brave Boy of the Waxshaws'. This late 19th-century print depicts, in suitably melodramatic form, how young Andrew received his scar and acquired a hatred of the British. (Marquis James,* **A Life of Andrew Jackson***)*

▶ *Andrew Jackson wearing the uniform he is reputed to have worn at New Orleans (it is now on display at the Smithsonian, Washington). Although not a 'gentleman', he was a general of consummate skill, and was the 'glue' that kept the polyglot American force together and turned it into a fighting machine. He was popular with some of his men, but, like Wellington, disdained popularity if it interfered with victory. (Anne S.K. Brown Military Collection, Brown University)*

appointment at not being appointed governor of the newly acquired Louisiana territory in 1803 was assuaged by the fact that Claiborne was. When the Arron Burr conspiracy was discovered and General James Wilkinson, one of the conspirators, turned state's evidence, Jackson, a friend of Burr's, was subpoenaed as a witness. However, his public condemnation of Wilkinson and his outspoken disapproval of President Jefferson led to his not being called.

When the war of 1812 was declared Jackson was desperate to fight the British, but now he had powerful enemies. These included all of Jefferson's friends, amongst whom was President James Madison. Jackson offered to lead 2,500 militia either to Canada or Florida, but the offer was refused. In October 1812 Dr William Eustis, the Secretary at War, asked for 1,500, without Jackson, to support General Wilkinson's invasion of West Florida. Jackson swallowed his pride and offered to serve under Wilkinson. This, plus his popularity with the men, tipped the balance; he and his men were ordered to Natchez to await further orders. With surprising administrative skill he kept his force in good order and completed his march in only 39 days during the cold January of 1813.

His 'further orders' arrived in March, although they were dated 6 February; they stated that the militia were either to disband and re-enlist as regulars or to make their own way home without transportation, food, or pay. Jackson had Wilkinson's recruiting parties thrown out of camp, and led his men the 800 miles back to Tennessee on foot, paying their expenses himself. On this march he gained the nickname 'Old Hickory' and the undying friendship of his men, including two colonels, John Coffee and William Caroll. Back in Nashville he fought another duel and was wounded. During his recovery he learned of the Creek Indian uprising and the massacre at Fort Mims on 30 August. Without waiting for State approval, he called out the militia and led them against the indians. His

leadership in the Creek war put him in the first rank of American Generals, but by forcing himself on campaign before fully recovering from his last duel, from which he still carried a ball in his shoulder, he permanently broke his health. For the rest of his life he was plagued by intestinal problems.

During the campaign the remarkable quality of Jackson's leadership, alone at times, kept his men in the field. They knew that there was no man in the Army tougher than the General. Jackson fought his first battle, and won his first victory, at Talladega on 9 November 1813. In January 1814, with a few reinforcements, he renewed his attacks, but on the 22nd at Entochopko Creek he was counterattacked, and

▲ *Brigadier General John Coffee, Commander of the Militia and indians who formed Jackson's extended left wing. In manning this position they spent several days* *permanently in the swamp, in the company of alligators and snakes. (Courtesy of the Louisiana State Museum)*

▲ *Major General William Caroll, Commander of the West Tennessee Militia. He* *later became Governor of Tennessee. (Courtesy of the Louisiana State Museum)*

his rear-guard fled. Only prompt action by Jackson, Caroll, and Coffee, the latter badly wounded, saved the day. David Crockett, who was fighting in the ranks of the militia that day, called the action a 'damned tight squeeze'.

Jackson, now in command of a force 5,000 strong, including a regiment of regulars, was about to strike at the heart of the Creek nation. To emphasise the seriousness of what they were doing, he had a deserter publicly executed and then marched his men off. At Horseshoe Bend he came up to the indian fort and, instead of laying siege to it, decided on a frontal assault. Although the Americans had high casualties, the attack succeeded. The power of the Creeks was broken, and they were forced to accept a humiliating treaty. This had a profound effect on the New Orleans campaign. Had the Creeks (who were British allies) been able to hold back their braves until late 1814, the British campaign in the south might have had a different outcome.

The choice of who was to defend the south was now obvious. Regardless of how much the Washington crowd disliked him, Andrew Jackson was transferred to the regular army as a Major General and given the command.

The rest of the American commanders, whether military, naval, or civil, can be seen only in the context of assisting or attempting to obstruct Jackson's plans. His active brain and iron will commanded every aspect of the American defence and campaign. Indeed, he was even writing to Claiborne on the subject in February 1813 while at Natchez awaiting Wilkinson's 'further orders'.

Separate mention should be made of two Frenchmen attached to Jackson's staff for the campaign.

The first was Arsene Lacarriere Latour, an émigré living in San Domingo when it was taken by the British. Like the brothers Lafitte, he chose to leave, and late in 1810 arrived in New Orleans as a refugee. He helped map the city and became a friend of Lafitte's, though whether or not they had known each other previously is open to question.

In 1813 Edward Livingston, supplementing his law practice by acting as one of Jackson's ADCs, introduced Latour to Jackson. Latour planned the defence works of Line Jackson and those of the West

▲ *General Humbert, ironically present at both the first and last battles of Pakenham's career.*

Bank, although his absence from the site of the latter works doubtless accounts for their poor construction. However, Latour's main contributions to the history of the battle are the book he wrote and the series of maps he produced (from which many of the maps in this book are drawn).

The second Frenchman, General Joseph Amable Humbert, was an advisor on Jackson's staff, and the commander of the abortive Irish expedition which had placed him on the same battlefield as Edward Pakenham once before. At one point Jackson wanted him to command his troops on the West Bank, but they refused to serve under a 'foreigner'.

# THE OPPOSING ARMIES

## The British Expeditionary Force

The British army mustered for the New Orleans campaign was the product of over 100 years of regimental tradition and success. They were masters of the linear tactics developed by Frederick the Great, and had proved themselves by defeating every army Napoleon had been able to throw at them. Their skill had made the British Empire the most far-reaching political and commercial entity the world was ever to know. The sphere of British involvement in the world was evident from the points of embarkation of the various regiments: Spain, France, Italy, South Africa and Jamaica.

The only cavalry on the expedition were the 14th Light Dragoons, converted from a standard dragoon regiment in the late 18th century. Their battle honours encapsulated their service under Wellington: Douro, Salamanca, Vittoria, Pyrenees and Orthes. They also fought at Toulouse, but did not receive the honour. They marched to Calais in July 1814 and crossed the Channel, and on the 21st they were reviewed by the Duke of York at Hounslow. In August they sailed to join the American expedition. They embarked without horses, expecting to be able to obtain mounts when they arrived, but the few horses available went to the staff and regimental commanders. The regiment formed part of Lambert's brigade, and was thus part of the reserve. During the withdrawal, one officer and 37 men were in one of the boats captured by the Americans, who were sailing under false colours, and they were subsequently used in prisoner exchanges.

The 4th Foot (The King's Own) was raised in 1680 by Charles II and therefore dates from the very beginning of the British Army. During the Napoleonic wars the regiment won battle honours at Corunna, Badajoz, Salamanca, Vittoria, San Sebastian and Nive. They marched to Bordeaux and took ship for America, where they gained yet another honour for Bladensburg under General Ross and took part in every action up to and including New Orleans.

The 7th Foot (Royal Fusiliers) were formed in 1685 as one of the regiments specifically designated to protect artillery trains, and were issued with the then new flintlock musket or 'fuzil'; hence their title. They were always a fashionable regiment, having certain uniform distinctions including a bearskin cap for full dress, and recruited from the London district. It was, of course, General Pakenham's old regiment.

Formed in 1678 as the Earl of Mar's Regiment, the 21st Foot was designated the North British Fusiliers in 1707 and received the title Royal in 1712. They saw service throughout the 18th century at Blenheim, Ramillies, Oudenarde, Malplaquet and Dettingen. During the Napoleonic wars they were on home service until 1807, when they went to Egypt, going to Sicily the following year to threaten the French, who were occupying the Kingdom of Naples. In 1811 they were sent to the east coast of Spain to assist Wellington in driving out the French. In 1813 they were sent to Genoa to assist in the removal of French troops from Italy. In 1814 they sailed direct to America, serving at Bladensburg, Washington and Baltimore. At the battle of New Orleans, Harry Smith of the Rifles, on Pakenham's staff as DAAG, expressed the opinion that the 21st and 44th lacked discipline.

The 43rd Foot (Monmouth Light Infantry) were one of the original light infantry regiments or 'Shorncliffe boys' as they were known, after the camp at which they were trained. After the new land-pattern musket was introduced their training was undertaken by General John Moore, who had trained himself to get off five shots per minute with the weapon, twice the rate of fire expected of line infantry. The light infantry not only took pride in their superior proficiency in musketry, but also in their self-sufficiency in providing themselves with food and shelter in the field.

The 44th Foot (East Essex Regiment) had had a creditable war, serving in Egypt with Abercrombie and later in the Peninsula at Badajoz and Salamanca. Along with the 4th Foot, after Napoleon's abdication, they embarked direct to the Americas. On the death of General Ross, Colonel Brooke took command of the army as senior officer present. By the time the regiment reached New Orleans command had devolved on Captain the Hon Thomas Mullins, who held the brevet rank of Lieutenant Colonel. The losses suffered on the campaign, miserable conditions, and the inexperience of their commander combined to bring disaster to the British attack.

Raised in 1793, the 85th Foot (Bucks Volunteers) Light Infantry were also veterans of the Peninsula, where their numbers had been so reduced by constant action that in 1811 they were sent home to recruit, arriving at Portsmouth with only 20 officers and 246 men. When they returned to the Peninsula in 1813 they were led by Lieutenant Colonel William Thornton, who commanded them at the siege of San Sebastian and the battles of Nivelles, Nive and Bayonne. On 30 May 1814 they left the Peninsula for America. The regiment fought in all the major actions of the war, and Thornton gained a reputation for his daring and for his intelligent leadership of his regiment and of the various battalions of detachments he was given. At Bladensburg he was wounded but recovered sufficiently to lead his regiment, and yet more detachments, at New Orleans.

Although embodied in October 1800, the 93rd Foot (Sutherland Highlanders) had been formed some time earlier as a fencible regiment. Their first posting was to Ireland in 1803, where they were kept to prevent the embers of rebellion, still smouldering after General Humbert's French expedition, from being fanned into flames. They not only succeeded, but also managed to become rather popular with the Irish, a remarkable accomplishment. In 1805 they were sent on the expedition to capture Cape Colony from the Dutch. Their baptism of fire was a great success and earned them a battle honour. Once again the regiment proved popular with the locals, being particularly intelligent and devout.

*Officer, 43rd Regiment. Illustration by Bryan Fosten.*

They provided teachers for schools that needed them, and set up a regimental church. Their distance from their supply base led to a shortage of kilts, and as a stop-gap measure kilts in good condition were re-made as trews for the entire regiment. The privates were also wearing their hummel bonnets without feathers, and it was in this attenuated Highland dress that they were ordered to join the American expedition.

Experience with specialist light troops in the American revolution, and the lack of such troops in the 1799 campaign in Holland, lead to the formation of 'the Experimental Corps of Riflemen' by Colonel Coote Manningham in 1800. Later the regiment entered the line as the 95th Foot (Rifles). From the start, the 95th were an élite unit because of their superior training and esprit de corps. Unlike the rest of the line, they were often used in small unconnected groups in situations that called for superior intelligence and an encyclopedic knowledge of the drill manual. Their orders were cut to a minimum on campaign. On the command 'halt' they would order arms and stand at ease with no further instruction. Similarly, the word 'march' would set them off at their quickest time, and all orders could be transmitted by bugle or whistle. After their involvement in the Peninsula they sailed directly for America, where they were involved in every action and covered themselves with as much glory as possible during a campaign of this nature. In 1816 they were taken out of the line and given the title 'The Rifle Brigade'.

In 1796 no less a person than Sir John Moore wrote: 'The Black Corps possess, I think, many excellent qualities and may, with proper attention, be equal to anything.' One of the units to which he was referring was Whytes Regiment, which in 1798 was gazetted as the 1st West India Regiment. By 1799 twelve regiments had been raised to garrison British possessions in the Caribbean, particularly Jamaica and Barbados. Initially there were some white privates, but the corps were chiefly composed of freed slaves with white officers. To begin with, NCOs were drawn from the regular army, but by 1810 negro soldiers were beginning to become corporals and sergeants and climb the ladder of promotion. The regiments gained battle honours at Dominica, Martinique and Guadeloupe, with the result that at New Orleans they were fighting alongside some old comrades.

## ORDER OF BATTLE: BRITISH ARMY

Commander-in-Chief, Major General Sir Edward Michael Pakenham, KB
Chief Engineer, Lieutenant Colonel John Fox Burgoyne, RE
Artillery Commander, Lieutenant Colonel Alexander Dickson, RA

### REGIMENTS PRESENT

| | |
|---|---|
| 14th Light Dragoons | 210 |
| 4th Foot | 796 |
| 7th Foot | 780 |
| 21st Foot | 790 |
| 43rd Foot | 862 |
| 44th Foot | 816 |
| 93rd Foot | 1,008 |
| 95th Foot (3rd Battalion) | 546 |
| 1st West India Regiment | 912 |
| 5th West India Regiment | 796 |

### DISPOSITION
**1st Brigade, Reserve**
Major General John Lambert
14th Light Dragoons, dismounted
7th Foot (Royal Fusiliers), minus Light Company

43rd Foot (Monmouth Light Infantry), minus one company
5th West India Regiment, minus Light Company

**2nd Brigade, Right Wing**
Major General Samuel Gibbs
Battalion of Light Companies under Colonel Jones attacking through cypress swamp.
4th, 44th, 21st and 5th West India.
4th Foot (Kings Own), minus Light Company
21st Foot (Royal Scots Fusiliers), minus Light Company
44th Foot (East Essex), minus Light Company carrying ladders and fascines.
95th Foot (Rifles) Detachment acting as skirmishers for column.

**3rd Brigade, Left Wing**
Major General John Keane
Battalion of Light Companies under Lieutenant Colonel Rennie.

7th, 93rd and 43rd
93rd Foot (Sutherland Highlanders), minus Light Company
1st West India Regiment
95th Foot (Rifles) Detachment acting as skirmishers for column.

*Total of British troops facing Line Jackson 6,970*

**Column of attack on the West Bank**
Lieutenant William Thornton, 85th Foot
85th Foot (Bucks Light Infantry)
Royal Marines    Detachment of 100
Sailors    Detachment of 100

*Total of British troops facing General Morgan 760*

▲ *A Rocket Troop of the Royal Horse Artillery on the march and in action, from the drill* *manual.(Anne S.K. Brown Military Collection, Brown University)*

Pakenham's Deputy Assistant Adjutant General, Captain (later Major General Sir) George de Lacy Evans, was nominally of the 5th West India Regiment, but the New Orleans expedition was the only time he served on the same field as his regiment.

The expedition was accompanied by two batteries of Royal Artillery and a rocket troop of the Royal Horse Artillery. Artillery, of course, goes so far back in British military history that it is difficult to put a definite date on its foundation, but the familiar blue coat was adopted in 1715 and the horse artillery raised in 1793. For a while, each artillery troop or battery carried its own battle honours, but this became so confusing that the Latin motto *ubique* (everywhere) was adopted. This motto certainly covers the service of the artillery, who even ended up in places where the rest of the British army was absent, such as the rocket troop that took part in the battle of Leipzig.

At New Orleans they were supplemented by the Royal Marine Artillery and by naval gunners.

Indeed, the nature of the campaign called for every man possible, whatever his arm of service, to help with the job in hand, whether it be manoeuvring a naval gun over muddy ground, damming a creek, or storming an enemy position.

## The American Defenders

Like all left-wing revolutionaries, Thomas Jefferson could not wait to gain power in order to try some hare-brained scheme or other. Despite his dictum that 'the tree of liberty needs watering with blood occasionally', his particular lunatic theory was that 'free men volunteering to defend their homes would always overcome the hirelings of a despot'. The practical application of this was that, on becoming President, to the horror of the opposition Federalist party, he (the Republicans) emasculated the army and navy.

In 1808 the army consisted of two regiments of infantry, one of artillery, and one General Officer, James Wilkinson, who from 1801 had been America's only regular army general. This little force was kept permanently in the South and particularly in the New Orleans area after 1803, because at that remove from Washington Wilkinson was better

*95th Rifles. Left to right: officer, rifleman and sergeant. Illustration by Bryan Fosten.*

▲ *An 1840 view of the battle, depicting the erroneous conception of how the cotton bales were used, not as foundations for the gun platforms but as the only defence. The unit depicted is probably the 7th Infantry, who gained the nickname 'The Cottonbailers' because of the battle. Although the regulars are shown in full dress of a later period, the riflemen in the background (over the crop of Jackson's horse) are surprisingly accurate.*

*(Courtesy of the Neal Auction Company, New Orleans)*

▶ *General James Wilkinson, until 1808 America's only General officer of the regular army, for whom double-dealing was a way of life. He treated the minuscule US Army as his personal property and kept it, and its funds, as near to himself as possible, which usually meant disease-ridden camps in the South. His diversion of*

*funds from New Orleans left local forts and vessels in poor repair. Several years after his death it*

*was discovered that he had been a spy for the Spanish. (Author's Collection)*

able to siphon off money meant for the army, and he could report all the easier to his Spanish paymasters.

In 1809 the army was expanded by one rifle, one light artillery, one light dragoon and five infantry regiments, and two more General Officers. Even so, there was no American staff to compare with the highly efficient British staff system. The field drill of the infantry and cavalry was rudimentary at best. However, the artillery and engineers were efficient and skilled, and from their ranks came many of the future generals.

▲ Major Jean Baptiste Plauche is depicted as a militia general in about 1820 in this illustration, but it gives a good idea which army his 'Uniformed Battalion' used as its model. Indeed, it is probable that he imported the much-praised uniforms from Paris. Unfortunately for his corps, the British never came close enough to his position for them to inflict much (if any) damage. (Courtesy of the Louisiana State Museum)

▲ Michael Fortier, a wealthy planter who financed and organized the black troops of the New Orleans, though he did not command them in the field. Although some authorities have claimed that he was mulatto, he was in fact white. (Courtesy of the Louisiana State Museum)

The 7th Infantry was recruited from Kentucky. In their early existence they experienced the Wilkinson treatment, being posted to New Orleans, and camped on highly unsuitable ground, losing almost half their number to disease while their commander played at being a general. Later, though, they fought with Harrison in 1813 at Tippicanoe in Indiana and in 1814 at Prairie du Chine in Wisconsin. The regiment was then ordered to join Jackson at New Orleans.

The 44th Infantry was one of the additional regiments raised in 1813, when the American government realised that, in sowing the wind, they were likely to reap the whirlwind. The regiment was to join Jackson in 1814, and fought under him in the taking of Pensacola on 7 November; they then marched to New Orleans to take part in the defence.

Naturally, members of the Corps of Artillery were involved in the action, but the rest of American army at New Orleans were militia. The local militia varied in quality, the best being the uniformed battalion of Major Jean Baptiste Plauche and Major Pierre Lacoste's battalion of Louisiana Free Men of Colour.

▶ *An American Militia regiment drawn up from a Militia drill manual of 1817. The theory and the practice generally differed greatly. (Author's Collection)*

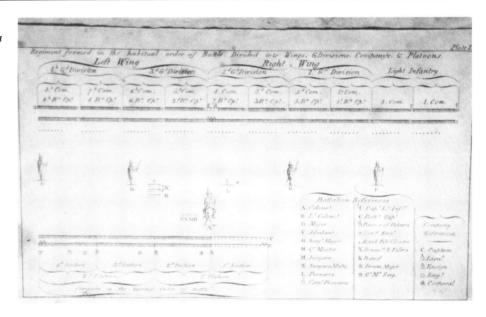

Despite the many references to Plauche's battalion's wonderful uniforms, no contemporary descriptions exist. However, there is strong circumstantial evidence that they were imported from France and closely resembled the undress uniforms of the Imperial or National Guard.

The Free Men of Colour were formed under the Spanish, and certainly were originally equipped in the white colonial uniform. They were not originally wanted by the new administration, but Claiborne gave them his support. With the fall of San Domingo more free wealthy negroes came to New Orleans, and a second company of Free Men of Colour was formed under Major Louis Daquin.

Many other groups of regular and irregular militia were formed in the area in the period before the battle. Most had no uniform whatsoever, and used their civilian clothes. Others had rudimentary uniforms made for them by quickly running up hunting shirts of uniform colour, some sky blue with a white fringe, some blue-and-white check.

Most of the units were basically groups of friends or members of the same clubs with no interest in soldiering, and were unable to obtain the blue coats, black shakos, belts, or white trousers laid down in militia regulations.

## ORDER OF BATTLE: AMERICAN ARMY

Commander-in-Chief, Major General Andrew Jackson
Chief Engineer (volunteer) Arsene Lacarriere Latour

**Regular Troops**

| | |
|---|---|
| Regular Light Artillery | 78 |
| 7th US Infantry | 436 |
| 44th US Infantry | 352 |
| United States Marines | 58 |
| One Troop 1st US Dragoons | 52 |
| Total | 976 |

**Louisiana Militia and Volunteers**

| | |
|---|---|
| Plauche's Uniformed Militia | 315 |
| Lacoste's Free Men of Colour | 282 |
| Daquin's Free Men of Colour | 180 |
| Baratarians (pirate gunners) | 36 |
| Jugeat's Choctaws | 62 |
| Total | 910 |

**Other Militia**

| | |
|---|---|
| Caroll's Tennessee Riflemen (11 companies) | 806 |
| Coffee's Tennessee Riflemen (9 companies) | 546 |
| Adair's Kentucky Riflemen (10 companies) | 680 |
| Total troops on Line Jackson with 14 guns | 3,918 |

**Reserve**

| | |
|---|---|
| Hind's Mississippi Mounted Rifles | 150 |
| Ogden's troop 1st US Dragoons | 50 |
| Harrison's bn Kentucky Militia | 306 |
| Total Reserve | 506 |

**Troops on the West Bank under General Morgan**

| | |
|---|---|
| Naval battalion, Commodore Patterson | 106 |
| Louisiana Militia, Major Paul Arnaud | 250 |
| Kentucky Militia, Lieutenant-Colonel John Davis | 320 |
| Reinforcements sent by Jackson | 400 |
| Total, with 16 guns | 1,076 |

The militia regiments from Kentucky and Tennessee were in the same state of dress, except that many of them had been off fighting the Creek Indians with Jackson and were consequently dishevelled, to say the least. However, they did have unswerving loyalty to a commander in whom they believed. This experience of the hardships of campaign was invaluable to them.

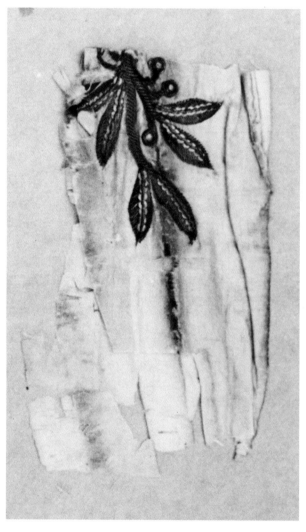

▲ *A fragment of the colour of Plauche's Uniformed Battalion. By tradition, the colour was divided amongst the members of the battalion after the battle; whether this happened immediately after, or on the dissolution of the battalion in later years, the fragments that survive in the families of those who were present at the battle are treasured mementoes. Unfortunately, no illustration seems to have been made of the colour before it was divided. (Private Collection)*

*Private, US Light Dragoons. Just how many troopers of the regular dragoons actually received this uniform is unclear; certainly a large cache of unissued helmets was discovered in storage a while ago, so many museums have examples. The officers were probably still wearing the earlier Tarleton or cocked hat. The volunteer cavalry wore what they had to hand. Illustration by Bryan Fosten.*

# INITIAL ENCOUNTERS

## The British Arrive

The best description of the tortuous route that had to be taken by every soldier and all supplies from the transports to the British camp is in the journal of Colonel Alexander Dickson, RH. Of course, the army had been taken by boat from the fleet to Pea Island, and spent a day or so on that windswept marshy desert without cover before being transported to the landing site.

'When we left the "Anaconda",' Dickson wrote, 'the current was still favourable, the night very clear, but piercingly cold. The boats continued to row all night, and there cannot be said too much in favour of the... gig-men who by daylight... pulled at least 70 miles without intermission. The cold was excessive as it froze very hard, and a breeze served to make it more cutting, this wind was against us till daylight, when we found ourselves at no great distance from the land some miles to the northward of the entrance of the creek.

'The coast was nothing but high reeds to the edge of the water and therefore unfit and impracticable to land upon. Or at least to move for many yards, being a deep swamp. After running along the coast, (the appearance of which was almost the same) for four or five miles, we made the entrance of the creek which was only discoverable from the rest of the coast by a red flag our people had hoisted on a pole as a land mark.

'On reaching the mouth we [followed]... the turns of the bayou, the banks of which on each side like the rest of the coast being covered with high and waving reeds, and here and there a short stubby tree or bush growing out of the bank.

'The creek has a great many turns and reaches in it and the whole way up is covered on each side by high reeds, it is of a good breadth for four or five miles, and then narrows so much, and is so shallow, that the boats cannot row for want of room and are pushed through the mud by means of the oars shoving against the bank.

'About a mile above the huts [Admiral Cochrane's headquarters] there are two broad creeks one running into the marsh on the right [the continuation of bayou Bienvenue] and the other to the left [bayou Mazant], and all the way up there are on both sides a number of little channels and inlets, full of water, which would render moving along the bank impossible, even where it is hard enough.

'From the landing place to headquarters is about 2½ miles, the road being nothing more than a very bad and boggy path along the bank of a little canal... which extends from the creek nearly to the Mississippi and is navigable with canoes to within 1,000 yards of the river. This is named Bayou Villare [bayou Villeré] being for the use of the plantation.

'The road for a distance of ¾ of a mile from the landing place is through reeds and the ground consequently very boggy, it then enters a thick wood about 1¼ miles across... the wood is generally of cypress trees growing closely together and full of thick brush and palmettos the bottom being swampy with deep holes interspersed, full of water, it is therefore in every respect impracticable.

'From the edge of the wood to Villares' [Villeré's] Plantation the distance is about half a mile of tolerably good and broad road, and from the plantation to the bank of the river is about 300 yards. A party is employed in improving this road.'

Dickson made this journey on 25 December, but on the night of the 22nd the same journey had been undertaken by General Keane and the advance party of the British invasion force. As they entered bayou Bienvenue the Spanish fishermen who had offered to help Cochrane pointed out the landing place for their village, where the one sick man who had been left behind had told the six American scouts who had arrived earlier that the rest of the men were out on a fishing trip.

At 0400 on the 23rd all but one of the scouts sent by Major Villeré were asleep and the one guard was not alert. In a matter of minutes sailors had captured the village. Four of the Americans managed to escape, three being captured that night and the other taking three days to reach the city, by which time his news was out of date.

The Expedition continued towards the plantation of General Villeré, the leading boats containing the 3rd Battalion of the 95th Rifles. When they came ashore at 0900 and started to advance upon the plantation house, they were amazed to find no pickets. It became obvious that attack was far from the mind of Major Gabriel Villeré. He and his company of 30 militia were surrounded, surprised and captured. The Major himself was captured on the veranda of his father's house, enjoying a morning cigar.

Villeré's ignoring of Jackson's direct order to block the canal on his family property had placed him in an invidious position, for if he were to escape and warn Jackson of the British presence, he also had to admit his own culpability in the affair.

When the entire advance guard of the 95th, 4th, and 85th had arrived and scouted the surrounding area, finding no enemy, troops, or even pickets, they were ordered to make camp and rest. The fatigues of the night told on the British, not least on the soldiers guarding Gabriel Villeré. Seizing his opportunity, the Major jumped from the window of the room where he was being held, vaulted the plantation fence, and sprinted over the fields. The pickets fired at him but missed, and he vanished in the direction of the De La Ronde house.

At his neighbour's he found De La Ronde, who was both the colonel of his militia regiment and his father-in-law. He had already sent Jackson word of the British arrival. The two decided to report to Jackson direct, but rowed across the river to find horses with which to reach headquarters instead of just riding down the river road to the city.

## Jackson Reacts

As De La Ronde and Villeré galloped down the west bank, Major Howell Tatum, who had arrived on the plantation just after their departure, was posting back on the other side of the river. When the first report of British troops reached Jackson he did not put much credence in it, but sent Major Tatum and his engineer Latour to investigate. By the time they reached the Bienvenue plantation they met people fleeing to New Orleans, saying that the British had arrived and had already captured the Villeré plantation.

As he waited for news, General Jackson did not commit his troops in any particular area. They were scattered to cover all the main approaches to the city, but in readiness to concentrate at any given point on his order.

◀ *The Villeré plantation house, where Gabriel Villeré was captured and escaped, and which later became General Pakenham's headquarters. This old photograph was taken before the house was demolished to make way for a sewage farm. (Marquis James,* **The Life of Andrew Jackson***)*

Latour remained at the Bienvenue plantation to continue his reconnaissance, while Tatum reported back. The refugees were already in the city by the time Tatum reported to Jackson, and he arrived only a few minutes before De La Ronde and Villeré (who had rowed back across the river to reach the city) muddy, dishevelled and shouting a stream of unintelligible French. By 1400 Latour's reconnaissance report was in Jackson's hands; the engineer estimated a force of between 1,600 and 1,800; obviously not the entire invasion force. Jackson relieved Villeré of his sword and placed him under arrest for not blocking his waterway as ordered.

Jackson still clung to the idea that his enemy would advance overland to cut him off from Baton Rouge in the north, and was unwilling to gamble that this would be the landing place of the main force. Consequently, he sent Claiborne (who as Governor was also General of the State Militia) with the 1st, 2nd and 4th Louisiana Militia, and a volunteer mounted company to hold the Chief Menteur/ Gentilly area where he expected the main landing.

▲ *Dennis De La Ronde, wearing the uniform of an officer of the Spanish Colonial Militia. He joined his son-in-law in a mysterious visit to the West Bank of the Mississippi before informing Jackson of the arrival of the British. Why he and Gabriel Villeré did not ride directly to the city has never been fully explained. (Benson Lossing's* Field Book of the War of 1812*)*

▶ *Versailles, the De La Ronde plantation house captured by the British and used as a forward headquarters by General Gibbs. (Benson Lossing's* Field Book of the War of 1812*)*

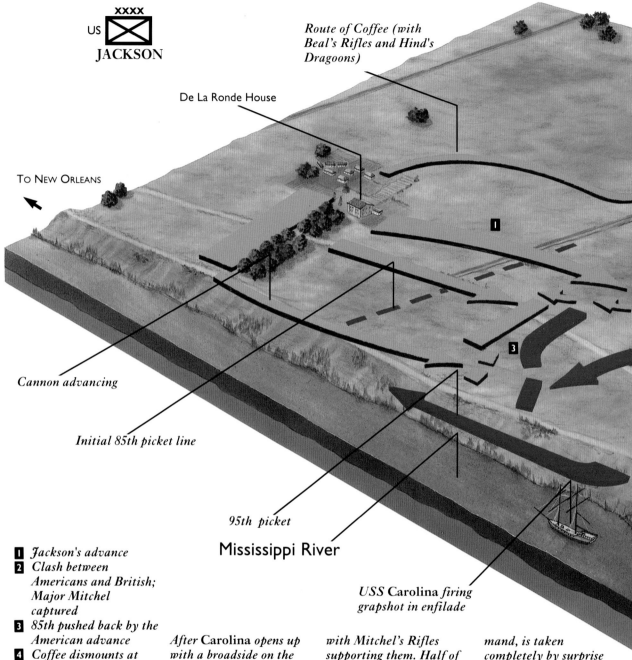

US **JACKSON**

Route of Coffee (with Beal's Rifles and Hind's Dragoons)

De La Ronde House

To NEW ORLEANS

Cannon advancing

Initial 85th picket line

95th picket

**Mississippi River**

USS Carolina firing grapshot in enfilade

1 Jackson's advance
2 Clash between Americans and British; Major Mitchel captured
3 85th pushed back by the American advance
4 Coffee dismounts at canal
5 Coffee returns to Jackson
6 Beal's riflemen get lost
7 British counter-attack by 85th and 95th reinforcements
8 Arrival of 21st
9 4th Foot (reserve)

After Carolina opens up with a broadside on the British camp, exactly as planned, the attack and defence becme hopelessly confused. Jackson's centre and right become inter-mingled with Daquin's battalion of Free Men of Colour, stumbling into the piquets of the 85th with Mitchel's Rifles supporting them. Half of Jackson's men get lost in the darkness and end up in the British camp, where they take a few prisoners before the majority are captured by the arriving 21st Foot.

Meanwhile Kean, in his first independent com-mand, is taken completely by surprise and is unable to organize a defence. Colonel Thornton of the 85th somehow manages to organize a defence and a counter-attack but has no idea how many men the enemy have or what their objective might be.

# THE NIGHT BATTLE OF 23 DECEMBER

**Jackson's three-pronged attack on the east bank, late evening of 23rd to the early morning of 24th**

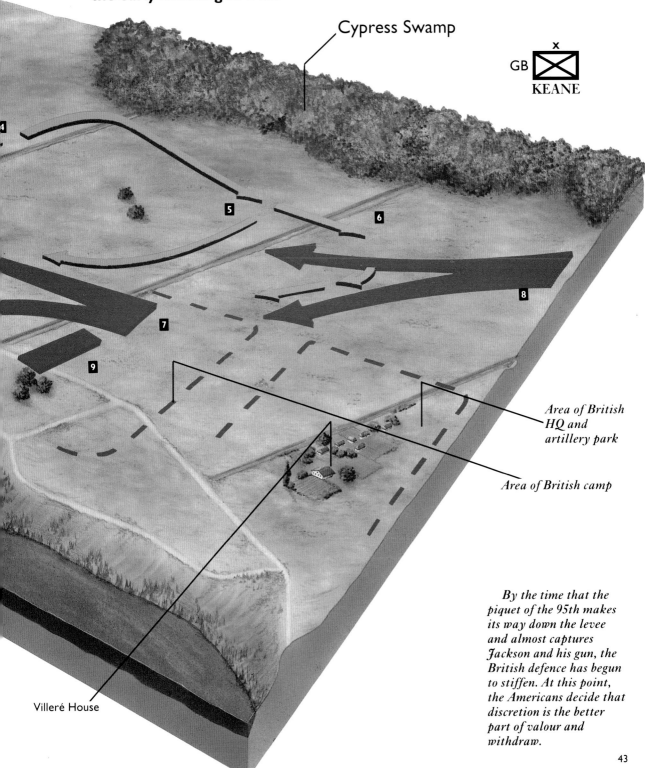

Cypress Swamp

GB KEANE

4

5

6

7

8

9

Area of British HQ and artillery park

Area of British camp

Villeré House

*By the time that the piquet of the 95th makes its way down the levee and almost captures Jackson and his gun, the British defence has begun to stiffen. At this point, the Americans decide that discretion is the better part of valour and withdraw.*

Meanwhile, he gathered together his main force of Tennesseeans under Caroll, camped four miles above the city, and mobilised the 7th Infantry under Major Henry B. Petere and a detachment of two 6pdr guns. He had already dispatched his Inspector General, Arthur P. Haynes, forward to continue reconnoitring the British position, and Major Thomas Hind's Mississippi Dragoons, accompanied by Captain Thomas Beal's New Orleans Rifles, to screen the movements of the American force.

They reached their position by 1500, but as the British pickets opened fire on them in the area of the De La Ronde plantation, they fell back out of rifle range. By 1600 the Tennesseeans were in position as the advance guard at the Rodriguez Canal, and within the next hour the 44th Infantry plus Major Plauche's battalion, a company of Choctaw Indians under Captain Pierre Jugeant, and Daquin's Free Men of Colour had joined the 7th at Fort St Charles to await orders.

Commodore Patterson was ordered to take the *Carolina* down river as silently as possible until he was opposite the British position and then open fire. The plan, a three-pronged co-ordinated assault at night, was very ambitious.

## The Night Battle

After the excitement of capturing the militiamen at the plantation, the British advance guard settled down to a comfortable afternoon. For the first time in weeks the weather was warm and dry, and they were on land. On their arrival General Keane had sent the 4th, 85th and 95th up river in three columns as far as the Lacoste plantation, and had a detachment of 100 men go down river to secure his rear. This rearguard discovered the force of General Morgan, but could not determine how strong it was as it retreated quickly before them.

While the camp was resting, the outposts at Lacoste's plantation came into contact with Hind's' Dragoons. The skirmishers withdrew to line as the advance guard deployed, and a volley sent the horsemen scuttling off. Some of the British officers were elated by this, and now fully expected a repeat of Bladensburg. Others were not quite so sure, but while daylight lasted, no more Americans were seen.

At his headquarters in Villeré's mansion, Keane was feeling a little more secure, if not entirely confident. The Americans had shown a marked reluctance to engage him, so the important thing was to rest his exhausted men in preparation for what was

◄ *The 'Battle Flag' of Captain James Moore's Company of Tennessee Militia. This colour was carried during the night battle of 23 December and during subsequent actions. It was preserved until the early 1860s, when this engraving was made, but is now unfortunately lost. (Benson Lossing's* Field Book of the War of 1812*)*

► *A Baker rifle captured during the night battle. It is marked up to the 3rd Battalion of the 95th, and bears an engraved brass plate. (Courtesy of the Louisiana State Museum)*

to come. With the pickets posted, they were stood down. Darkness fell at about 1730.

The camp was still at ease at 1930, when the pickets of the 95th posted on the levee saw a vessel drifting towards them. The soldiers assumed it was a supply ship from the fleet and hailed it several times, but received no reply, even after it had dropped anchor. Suddenly the vessel, the USS *Carolina*, opened up with a broadside of grapeshot. The camp was in turmoil while officers frantically tried to assemble their commands for a counterattack, although in the dark no one was immediately certain from where the attack was coming.

Colonel Thornton took command of the situation, ordering the 95th to reinforce the pickets and the 85th to extend to cover the British left, and withdrawing the 4th to form a reserve.

Captain William Hallen of the 95th, commanding the picket on the levee, ordered his men to take cover as the broadside continued. Presently he noticed an American force supported by two guns moving up the levee road, driving in the inner picket of the 85th and extending to their right to take the ground the British were abandoning.

Other muzzle flashes from smallarms showed that the fighting had spread further inland. Actually, this was the relieving force of 85th and 95th, under the command of Major Samuel Mitchel, the senior rifleman on the expedition, which had been caught in flank almost by accident by supporting American troops. The British fell back slightly and re-formed ranks, from which they kept up steady volleys, but not before Major Mitchel had been captured.

From his position, Captain Hallen saw that the main threat lay in the guns that the Americans were moving up, and ordered his men to attack them. In the darkness the small group of riflemen almost succeeded. Colonel Thornton led the relieving force forward again, and the troops supporting the guns began to fall back. Just when it looked as though the guns would be taken, the Americans rallied, drove back the British, and saved them.

Now there was a threat to the British right. Sporadic firing could be heard from the rearguard pickets, but the 4th were now formed as a reserve at the Villeré house ready to meet the threat. A party of American riflemen had penetrated the camp and taken several prisoners, but at this moment the guns of the *Carolina* fell silent, and the British right was suddenly reinforced by men of the 21st Foot, who had just arrived from the fleet. They had heard the *Carolina*'s first broadside while still 20 miles away,

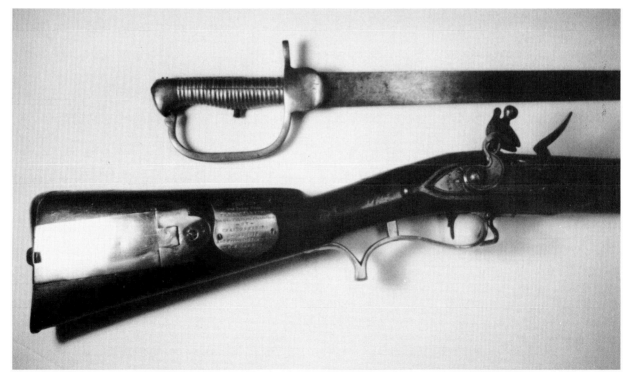

*Left to right: Sergeant, Grenadier Company, 93rd Regiment of Foot; Private, 5th West Indian Regiment; Officer, 1st West Indian Regiment. Illustration by Bryan Fosten.*

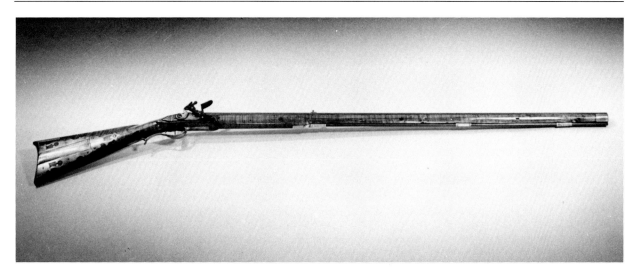

and the sailors had strained every muscle to get them to the field.

Now Americans withdrawing with British prisoners were themselves made captive. The attacking force withdrew into the night as a thick, wet, Mississippi fog covered the field. Apart from the sound of the popping muskets of over-enthusiastic Americans that continued well after midnight, the action was over. One unexpected bonus was the capture of several riderless American horses for the staff.

### The American Attack

Jackson's attack had been almost foolhardily ambitious: a three-pronged attack of independent commands, one of them naval, carried out at night. His left wing was composed of Coffee's mounted Tennessee riflemen and Beal's New Orleans riflemen with Hind's Dragoons. The right wing was Patterson in the *Carolina*, mounting a broadside of five 6pdrs and two swivel-mounted 12pdrs, one in the stern and one in the bow, all manned by expert gunners of Lafitte's band. Jackson commanded the centre with the 7th and 44th Infantry, Plauche's battalion, Daquin's battalion, and the New Orleans uniformed militia under Colonel George T. Ross. He placed his two guns on the right where they could quickly be run down the levee road under the protection of a detachment of Marines and 7th Infantry.

As soon as he received confirmation from Hind's Dragoons that this was indeed the British landing

*▲ A rifle used in the night battle of 23 December. The patchbox is engraved: 'This rifle was used by my father Wm Ross member of Cap. Thom's Beal's company of New Orleans Riflemen in the defence of N.* *Orleans 1814–1815 James Ross 1835.' This is the only fully documented weapon of this unit known to exist, and was used throughout the campaign. (Courtesy of the Robert Melancon Collection)*

site, and not just a feint, Jackson put his plan into action. All units were to be in place by 1930, at which time the signal for the attack was to be the sound of the first broadside from the *Carolina*. The *Carolina*'s crew were ordered to keep firing until they heard the distinctive sound of American long rifles, and then to cease fire for fear of hitting their own men.

The cavalry on the left wing, supported by Beal's rifles, was to be used to turn the British flank. The river attack would presumably drive the British inland while keeping their attention on the river. The dragoons and riflemen would then attack from the landward side, at which time the ship's guns would fall silent. Jackson would then advance up the centre and use his main force to drive them from the plantation buildings and, hopefully, into a precarious defensive position from which they would be forced to re-embark.

As darkness fell and the *Carolina* drifted slowly downstream, the first part of his plan was going perfectly. By 1930 he was in position, and the *Carolina*'s broadside heralded the start of the action right on time. As Jackson advanced, the guns were forcing the pickets back, and the 7th, extending to cover the ground, screened the gunners while they ran their pieces up.

On the left, however, things had broken down. Beal's men were supposed to be protecting the left flank of Coffee's horsemen, but, as more-or-less untrained civilians in their first action, they had become separated and had advanced well into the Villeré plantation.

Now things began to go wrong on the right. Although it appeared that the pickets had been driven in, the guns suddenly came under fire from the other side of the old levee road, down which they were being advanced. Almost simultaneously the centre all but fell over a party of British infantry heading in their direction. After some hand-to-hand fighting in which the commander of the party (Major Mitchel) was captured, the forces separated, but every now and then more groups of British would charge them. The American force began to close to the centre, and the guns were in grave danger.

On the left, Coffee had halted his men at the small canal that formed the boundary between Lacoste's and Villeré's plantations, dismounted, and marched his men towards the sound of the fighting. Some of the more adventurous decided to advance on the British camp instead, and became embroiled in a general mêlée. In the confusion some of the horses from both Hind's and Coffee's command galloped off and were captured by the British.

General Jackson, always at his best in a crisis, rallied the 44th and the militia to the support of the 7th and the marines protecting the guns just as yet another charge came at them. The British were narrowly beaten back, and the guns were saved. For a time Jackson was within 20 paces of the enemy.

Twenty-four of Beal's men, hopelessly lost, were returning to their lines when they came across some unarmed British soldiers and took them captive, continuing merrily on their way until they, in turn, were captured by other British infantry.

Coffee thought he had lost 200 of his men and all of Beal's rifles, but only 63 were captured or killed, and half of Beal's men made their way back during the night.

Jackson withdrew. The fighting was getting too confused, and in any case he considered he had won a qualified victory. American losses were 24 killed, 115 wounded, and 74 missing. Planning a renewed attack for the following day, he sent for Caroll's Kentucky brigade.

In his plans, though, Jackson seems to have completely forgotten about General David B. Morgan and his 350 Louisiana Militia down river of the British position. With no orders, Morgan sat at his post at English Turn while the battle raged, and refused to move until his men threatened to go without him. He led them as far as Jumonville's plantation, where the outlying pickets of the British fired on them. Morgan halted his men, sat in a muddy field until 0300, and then retreated to his original post. It was not only the Grand Old Duke of York who could march his men up and down to no effect. In the opinion of at least one of his men, Morgan was 'an old woman'.

At 0400 Jackson continued his retreat to the disused millrace that divided the Macarté and Chalmette plantations and had the rather grandiose name of the Rodriguez Canal. The action was at best a draw for the Americans but, now that the British were being reinforced here, Jackson felt that the chance of another landing elsewhere was minimal. He could therefore begin concentrating his troops on the narrow strip of land between the river and the swamp.

## Missed Opportunity?

Throughout the rest of the night, the remainder of the brigade commanded by Colonel Brooke of the 44th came ashore. The 21st, which had arrived during the battle, was followed by the 93rd and the 1st and 5th West India Regiments. By the time these last two regiments came ashore, 200 of their number had died of the cold on Pea Island or on the boat trip. In the British camp there were 46 dead and 167 wounded, with 64 missing.

Even Peninsula veterans were horrified by the terrible wounds inflicted by the US navy's grapeshot. It has been claimed, even by people present during the campaign, that this was due to the Americans' use of an improvised grapeshot of old locks, horseshoe nails, etc. This, of course, is pure fantasy; such articles would do as much damage to the cannon as it would to the enemy. Furthermore,

Jackson's agreeing to a pardon for the pirates centred on their ability to supply ammunition. It should be remembered that the only first-hand account of this comes from a militiaman writing 40 years after the battle. Sustained volleys of grape at close range were quite devastating enough to cause the wounds described.

The landing of the troops was finally completed by nightfall on 24 December. Here it is necessary to answer the charge that General Keane should have marched on the city as soon as he was ashore, and that his failure to do so lost the campaign on the night of the 23rd. Firstly, the only troops available to him were Thornton's brigade, with a total strength of 1,841 men, this total not taking into account the sick who had to be left behind. Secondly, he was not supposed to be in command in any case. Thirdly, he had learned from prisoners, runaway slaves, and the Spanish fishermen that he was facing an enemy of anything up to 15,000 strong, the location of which was anybody's guess. To string out his command in an advance on the city under these circumstances would have been foolish in the extreme.

## American Defences

As Jackson began pulling together his forces, he had the quite brilliant idea of sending forward a party to cut the levee between his position and the British. He also sent word to General Morgan at English Turn to do the same. Predictably, Morgan's cut was not deep enough, and was soon discovered and repaired, but Jackson, who had noticed that the river was higher than usual, now had 30in of water on the plain in front of him, preventing the possibility of attack while he prepared his defences. The original ditch was being dug out to 4ft deep and 12ft wide, the excavated earth creating a rampart 4ft high. This, in turn, was reinforced by the addition of wood on its face to stop the earth falling back into the ditch. The wood for this came from all the fences in the area.

On the river flank of the line a disused brick kiln was turned into a gun platform and redoubt. In addition to this, on the West Bank of the river (which at this point is geographically south because of a large meander) Jackson had created another defence work. Again the levee was cut by a ditch

▲ *General Morgan in an heroic pose that belies his actions during the night battle, and subsequently.* *(Courtesy of the Louisiana State Museum)*

and bared by an earthwork, but this work was a little downstream and was continued along the river bank back towards Jackson's position, providing a gun position from which any column attempting to use the levee road to assault his position could be raked in flank.

Guns were, in fact, the main defence for Line Jackson, as the Rodriguez Canal was now called, and Lafitte had been as good as his word in supplying powder shot and smallarms. He also provided two gun crews under his brother, Dominique You. The city and surrounding plantations had been cleared of all digging implements, and every soldier was put to the task of working on Line Jackson. This did not go down well with some of the soldiers, particularly the aristocratic creoles of the uniformed militia, who objected mightily to doing 'slave' labour and felt great resentment for their undoubtedly brave but uncouth 'American' commander.

In the days that followed, the sight of their sons, husbands and brothers attired for war but working like field hands also dismayed many of the citizens of New Orleans who made the eight-mile journey from the city to 'Line Jackson'. Some of these visitors, including members of the State Legislature, left the little mud wall of this American General who had never before fought anyone other than indians. They had no doubt that Wellington's Immortals would brush him aside like an annoying fly. The visitors could also see that the river was falling and the plain draining.

By 27 December it would be possible for the British to mount an attack. On the evening of the 27th, Colonel Alexander Declouet, who had been in command of his unit with General Morgan during the night battle on the 23rd, was inexplicably on leave and staying at the house of State Senator Magloire Guichard.

The two creoles fell into conversation on the prospects for the city if Jackson were to be defeated. Recently, more ships had arrived in New Orleans, including one moored in the city and closely guarded. Rumour had it that this vessel was packed with explosives which, in the event of defeat, Jackson would use to destroy the city. Declouet explained that there had been discussions amongst the officers of Morgan's command about Jackson

▼ *The preparation of 'Line Jackson'. Soldiers, tradesmen, militia, slaves and anyone who could wield a pick or spade, are put to work under Arsene Lacarriere Latour (on top of the works). The work was resented by the creole militia, who thought it beneath them, and it was thought pathetically inadequate by armchair generals visiting from the city, but it also built a comradeship between the men that paid off in the fighting. (Anne S.K. Brown Military Collection, Brown University)*

conducting a 'Russian Campaign', and that the city and their fortunes could be lost as a result. Guichard said that there had been a similar discussion amongst members of the State Legislature. Declouet asked for names.

Next morning the colonel rode towards Jackson's headquarters in the Macarté house just behind Line Jackson. As he approached he heard the sound of artillery; another battle had begun. Arriving on the field he saw Abner Duncan, Jackson's ADC, and, overtaking him at the gallop, shouted that he had important news for the General. Duncan pointed out Jackson's position, but Declouet insisted that Duncan take the message. The message was that the State Legislature were about to give up the country to the British.

## Pakenham Arrives

On Christmas day 1814 a British gun boomed a salute to welcome the Commander-in-Chief. Major General Sir Edward Pakenham, KB, had arrived. His journey from the fleet had been no less uncomfortable than anyone else's; in fact, the description of the journey by Colonel Dickson, RA, quoted earlier, was written as he accompanied General Pakenham to the British camp.

Pakenham's first impression was that his force was in a bottle and that they should re-embark and land elsewhere. However, officers of his staff who had been present at Bladensburg and Baltimore assured him that a determined advance with the bayonet was all that was needed to send American troops running.

The comment attributed to Admiral Cochrane on the reticence of General Pakenham to stage a frontal assault is derisory and insulting: 'If the army is afraid to face the dirtyshirts, then I will carry the position with my sailors, and the army can bring up the baggage!' It is not creditable that the courteous old Admiral would ever have used such words to General Pakenham. Indeed, this story seems to have been invented some years later, as no one who was present mentions it. However, it is possible that the Admiral gave his opinion of the American troops, which was not very high.

So the die was cast. The Americans would be engaged behind earthworks on a narrow strip of

*Officer, 1st Battalion, 85th Regiment of Foot. Despite the fact that the regiment had been campaigning in the north, frequent returns to the fleet and regrouping in Jamaica meant that a remarkable degree of regimental uniformity had been maintained. Illustration by Bryan Fosten.*

land, flat as a billiard table, with every soldier, cannon, musketball, and ounce of powder being rowed 64 miles from the British fleet. In spite of assurances, Pakenham still had his doubts.

However, he had no doubts that he wanted the American ships, the *Carolina* and *Louisiana*, which now had a crew, destroyed. His resolve had been strengthened by the *Carolina* constantly firing on the clearly marked British field hospital. These vessels posed an obvious threat to any move against Line Jackson.

Heavy siege artillery had not yet arrived, and the only guns available were battalion guns, a few 6pdrs, and some naval carronades manned by the Royal Marine Artillery, but Pakenham did have the artillery genius of Colonel Alexander Dickson. On the very day he arrived with the C-in-C, Dickson set up a furnace and began to fire on the American vessels with hot shot, cannon balls heated to cherry red before being fired. They made excellent incendiaries. The *Louisiana*, at extreme range, was taken out of range by her crew manning long boats and towing her, but the *Carolina* was hit and started blazing merrily. Her crew managed to evacuate her, even saving some of her guns, but she was totally destroyed.

Pakenham's lingering doubts about a frontal attack on a force behind earthworks were being eased by his Deputy Assistant Adjutant General, Captain de Lacy Evans, and Rear Admiral George Cockburn, who assured him of the same success General Ross had experienced at Bladensburg. However, Pakenham wanted to know more of his adversary before he committed himself irrevocably to a full-scale attack. He decided upon a reconnaissance in force. This would drive in Jackson's cavalry screen and give the artillery and engineers a view of the defence works so that its strong and weak points could be determined. Should the American defence waver whilst the operation was in progress, it would give him the opportunity to develop a full-scale attack.

### The Reconnaissance in Force

On the morning of the 28th everything was prepared, and the British moved off towards the American position. On the left, advancing down the levee road, was General Keane's brigade of light infantry, accompanied by Colonel Dickson with the light mortars and half of the RHA Rocket Troop under Captain Lane. On the right, Gibbs's brigade advanced with their flank to the cypress swamp, accompanying the 3pdr battalion guns and the other half of the Rocket Troop. At the rear of Gibbs's column marched the artillery reserve of two 9pdrs and four 6pdrs under Major John Mitchel. The advance

▲ *The Deputy Assistant Adjutant General, Captain George de Lacy Evans. A veteran of the Peninsular and Washington/Baltimore campaigns, Evans had gained a reputation for brilliant impetuosity when hopes were forlorn. Although he was on the field with the regiment in which he was nominally an officer (5th West India), he served only as a staff officer, in which capacity he was wounded. This print dates from the 1850s, by which time he had gained further fame in Spain and risen to the rank of Major General. He was to command a Brigade in the Crimea. At New Orleans he was 26. (Author's Collection)*

was screened by the 95th on the left and by the light companies of Gibbs's regiments on the right.

As the columns marched forward the American pickets withdrew, first from their advanced position at the De La Ronde plantation, then from their secondary position at the Bienvenue plantation, burning outbuildings and cane stubble as they left. The smoke was not as inconvenient for the British as it might have been; the morning was frosty and, although the sun had cleared the mist, it was unseasonably cold.

Because of the bend in the river and the smoking outbuildings of Bienvenue, the columns could not see Line Jackson until they had cleared the buildings and made a slight right wheel. At this point Keane's brigade was only 700 yards from the Americans as it deployed into line. Simultaneously, the four American land batteries, including two 24pdrs, opened up, as did the *Louisiana*, firing from the river. Initially, the only British reply was the rockets of Captain Lanes' detachment. However, in spite of Captain Gleig's somewhat hysterical account, stating: 'scarce a ball passed over its mark', and recalling 'terrible havoc' and 'shrieks of the wounded', according to Keane's report there were only 60 casualties.

The deployed brigade was then ordered to take cover as Dickson ordered up the artillery reserve from the rear of Gibbs's brigade. One 9pdr and a howitzer were placed on the levee to oppose the *Louisiana*, while the rest of the guns fired on Line Jackson. General Pakenham galloped up to Keane and ordered the infantry to stand fast and the artillery to continue firing; Dickson accompanied him back to Gibbs's brigade.

When they arrived on the right, Pakenham sent Lieutenant Peter Wright, RE, up a tree to reconnoitre the American position with a telescope and, dismounting, went forward on foot to examine the ground himself. When he returned, Lieutenant Wright reported that the ditch was filled with water and the swamp would be impassable by an attacking force. Pakenham then turned to Dickson and ordered him to bring up the artillery reserve. It appeared that battle was to be joined.

The plan was clear. Jackson's right was holding firm, supported by the guns of the *Louisiana* and the west bank battery, but the concentration of

▲ *George Robert Gleig, Lieutenant of the 85th Foot and author of* The Subaltern *and* Campaigns at Washington, *which includes an account of the New Orleans campaign. He subsequently took Holy Orders and became Chaplain General. (C. R. B.* Barrett, The 85th King's Light Infantry*)*

power against Keane's force had left Gibbs's brigade almost untouched. If Pakenham could support Gibbs with artillery, perhaps an attack could be mounted that would end the business immediately. He began to wait.

When Dickson arrived back at his artillery positions on the left, he found the situation deteriorating fast. Of the guns opposing the *Louisiana*, the two 6pdrs had had their carriages damaged and were out of action, forcing the 9pdr to withdraw to cover. Dickson started across the field with the 9pdr,

# The Reconnaissance in Force

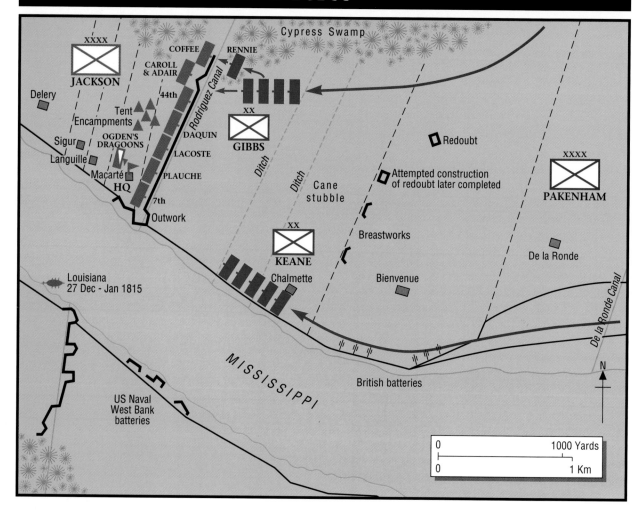

**Cypress Swamp**

XXXX
JACKSON

COFFEE
RENNIE
CAROLL & ADAIR
44th

Rodriguez Canal

Delery

Tent Encampments

Sigur
OGDEN'S DRAGOONS
Languille
Macarté
HQ

DAQUIN
LACOSTE
PLAUCHE
7th
Outwork

XX
GIBBS

Ditch

Ditch

Cane stubble

Redoubt

Attempted construction of redoubt later completed

XXXX
PAKENHAM

Breastworks

De la Ronde

XX
KEANE

Louisiana
27 Dec - Jan 1815

Chalmette

Bienvenue

De la Ronde Canal

US Naval West Bank batteries

MISSISSIPPI

British batteries

N

| 0 | 1000 Yards |
|---|---|
| 0 | 1 Km |

▲ *The tactics adopted by Pakenham for the reconnaissance in force were dictated by the nature of the ground, and were simple and direct. In spite of the numerical superiority of the American artillery, Jackson's weak left wing and the reputation of the British could have ensured victory if the attack had been pressed home.*

ordering Lieutenant Carmichael to follow with the two remaining sixes, and the laborious job of man-handling the guns over the muddy field began.

On the British right Pakenham ordered the troops of Gibbs's brigade to prepare earthworks for the guns, which were on their way. The Engineers found that digging to a depth of only 8in reached the water table. They toiled on, but there was still no sign of the guns. Finally, Pakenham decided that

he must wait for heavier guns and reinforcements; he ordered a general withdrawal.

Had he but known it, he had been on the point of victory. The advance guard of Gibbs' column had made contact with a detachment of Caroll's Kentuckians, which had been on outpost duty in the edge of the woods when the advance began. As they ran back to their position behind the rampart, they saw others leaving that position and running towards the centre. Perhaps their intention was to get a better shot at the British, but, for whatever reason, Jackson's left was giving way. At this very moment came the order to withdraw.

With bitter disappointment the men of the advance guard pulled back. A party of seamen and gunners manhandled the damaged artillery pieces back to the Villeré plantation, where ships' carpenters could repair them.

## Closing the Legislature

As his artillery started firing, Major General Andrew Jackson observed his line and wondered what would happen. He noticed that in some places the defences were too thin and balls could break through. However, the ground everywhere was so wet that the balls immediately buried themselves, reducing the danger.

▼ *The Place d'Armes, New Orleans, c.1830, looking as it did in 1815. On the left is the Cabildo, the seat of government, and on the right is the Presbytere, at that time a combination headquarters and gaol. In the centre is the St Louis Cathedral founded by the French in 1722 and rebuilt several times since. The troops on the left are, in all probability, Plauche's battalion looking for all the world like the Imperial Guard. The figure on horseback on the right, who looks like a French General, is probably Plauche himself. (Author's Collection)*

The British attacking his right were being held up, but his left seemed about to give way. Jackson had just ordered Jugeat's Choctaws to support his left and hold the swamp when he was halted by Abner Duncan, with the message from Colonel Declouet about the Legislature giving up the country to the enemy. Jackson ordered Duncan to ride to Governor Claiborne and order him to make immediate enquiries. 'If he finds out this is true,' said Jackson, putting spurs to his horse, 'tell him to blow up the Legislature!' Jackson arrived on his left at almost the same instant that the attack was halted.

Meanwhile, Duncan rode back to the city, into the Place d'Arms, and entered the Cabildo, where the Legislature sat. Governor Claiborne could not be found immediately and so, interpreting his orders quite freely, and using Jackson's authority, Duncan placed a guard on the entrance with the order that no one be allowed to enter.

It was just the hour when the Legislature was due to begin its sitting, and the Honourable Members were shocked to find their way barred by fixed bayonets. They were horrified when one of their number

attempted to force an entrance and was prodded with a bayonet by one of the guards, who told him that if he took one more step he would be run through.

After a brief but heated discussion, Senator Bernard de Marigny de Mandeville mounted his horse and, in a towering rage, rode off to confront this arrogant American General who had not only suspended the civil government but also had personally insulted him by spurning his offer of accommodation a few weeks earlier.

The British attack had taught Jackson a lot. It had shown him that his left was weak and that his rampart was not of sufficient size. The impression on the American force, though, was that they had just won a battle against Wellington's Invincibles – they had stopped the troops that beat Napoleon's best.

When Jackson returned to his headquarters he found Senator de Marigny waiting for him. It was only two hours since Abner Duncan had left the field. During his journey de Marigny had calmed down somewhat, and more so after arriving to find that he was to face a general who had just beaten the British. Jackson expressed sympathy for the Legislature's position and said that his orders had been misinterpreted, but he did not censure Captain Duncan. He also ventured to suggest that the Legislature could not distance themselves from the defence that he was conducting, and that, should the British succeed, the Legislature could expect a very hot time. De Marigny left as defused as a creole was capable of being.

## Constructing Line Jackson

It was time to prepare for the next attack. The hastily thrown up mud rampart varied in thickness between 5ft and 20ft, depending on the energy of its builders at any given point. Now it was reinforced and firing-steps were built to allow the defenders to shoot over the extra height.

Jackson had a stroke of genius. Although the Americans outgunned the British, they still had the problem of guns sinking into the sodden ground. He requisitioned 150 bales of cotton and put them in pits to give his batteries a firm footing. He also used them, covered in mud to prevent them catch-

▲ *Harry Smith of the 95th Foot, who took the news of the capture of Washington back to London and returned to America in the same ship as the new Commander in* *Chief. His experiences in the Americas, particularly at Buenos Aires and New Orleans, were not good, but after serving at Waterloo he went on to a brilliant career in India.*

ing fire, to construct a second rudimentary bastion at the edge of the wood where his flank had almost been turned.

To be doubly sure of securing the flank, which was beyond the range of both the west bank guns and the *Louisiana*'s broadsides, Latour advised him to extend the line into the cypress swamp. The new section extended for another half mile and then turned through 90 degrees for another 200 yards. The rampart here was made of fresh-cut logs placed 2ft apart, the centre being filled with earth. All this had to do was stop musketballs, as it would be impossible to bring artillery to bear on it. This section of the line was given to General Coffee with his Tennesseeans and the Choctaws.

Jackson realised that his main asset was his superiority in artillery, and called for every piece he could lay his hands on. By 31 December he had completed seven batteries containing one 32pdr, three 24pdrs, one 18pdr, three 12pdrs, three 6pdrs and a 6in howitzer. On the left bank he had two 24pdrs opposite the city, and he had the *Louisiana*

land its two 12pdrs for the battery flanking the levee. As a further protection for his left flank, parties of Tennesseeans, the troops who had been given the nickname 'dirtyshirts' by the British, were organised into 'hunting parties'. They sallied forth into the swamp to kill or drive in any pickets they might find.

For the British forces things still did not look good. The supply of ammunition for the artillery was nowhere near adequate, and by now Pakenham was convinced that artillery was what he needed. With artillery he could destroy Line Jackson's batteries. With the batteries out of action and the defences damaged, the infantry could sweep the Americans aside.

But there were many drawbacks. The difficulty of transporting guns from the fleet and manoeuvring them with muscle power and the few horses that had been captured meant that a heavy siege train was out of the question. Indeed, it was almost miraculous that Dickson had been able to bring up 18pdrs on their unwieldy naval carriages. The weather was wet and miserable, and the troops were becoming more and more disheartened. Even troops newly ferried

▼ *The Macarté House, Major General Jackson's headquarters throughout the battle, from a daguerreotype taken before the Civil War. The house fell into disrepair and finally caught fire,* *but substantial ruins existed until the land was removed to create a slipway for a local factory. (Marquis James's* Life of Andrew Jackson*)*

# The Artillery Battle

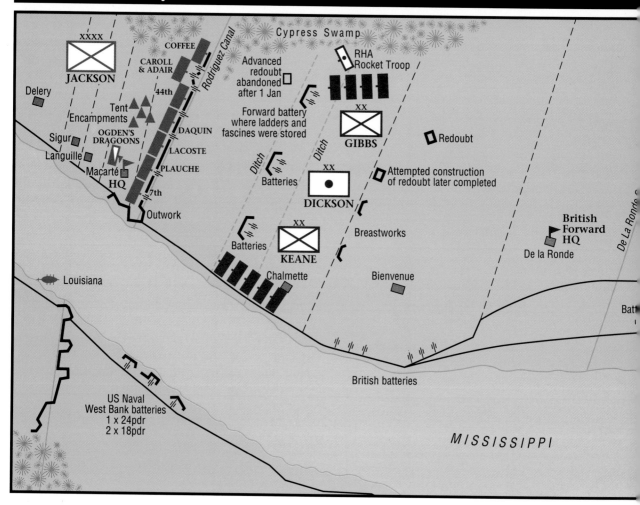

*Map labels:* XXXX JACKSON · COFFEE · CAROLL & ADAIR · 44th · Rodriguez Canal · Advanced redoubt abandoned after 1 Jan · RHA Rocket Troop · Cypress Swamp · Delery · Tent Encampments · OGDEN'S DRAGOONS · DAQUIN · LACOSTE · PLAUCHE · Forward battery where ladders and fascines were stored · XX GIBBS · Redoubt · Sigur · Languille · Macarté HQ · 7th · Ditch · Batteries · XX DICKSON · Ditch · Attempted construction of redoubt later completed · Outwork · Batteries · XX KEANE · Breastworks · British Forward HQ · De la Ronde · De La Ronde · Louisiana · Chalmette · Bienvenue · US Naval West Bank batteries 1 x 24pdr 2 x 18pdr · British batteries · Batt · MISSISSIPPI

in arrived exhausted, as they had to carry artillery ammunition in their packs. When one transport capsized in Lake Bourgne, the soldiers in it, who had been carrying cannon balls, sank without trace, much to the dismay of their comrades.

On 30 December, Pakenham sent Lieutenant Wright (who had climbed the tree on the 28th) off through the swamp to reconnoitre the enemy position. He did not return. Some British soldiers disappeared without being sent on a mission, though not many. These were principally from the 21st and 44th who, according to Harry Smith, were 'not distinguished for discipline'. The night of the 31st was particularly miserable for Colonel Dickson and the men working on the artillery positions.

## The Artillery Duel

Pakenham had decided to attack on New Year's Day 1815, and it had been decided that constructing the batteries at night would shield their positions from the Americans and protect the workers from artillery fire. The finished positions were far from satisfactory. As previously explained, the nature of the ground prevented the artillery from being dug in, so the main protection consisted of sugar barrels filled with earth, and the platforms were loose and uneven.

Still more seriously the 18pdrs, the heaviest of the British guns, were mounted on sea carriages not designed for land use, and ammunition was still in

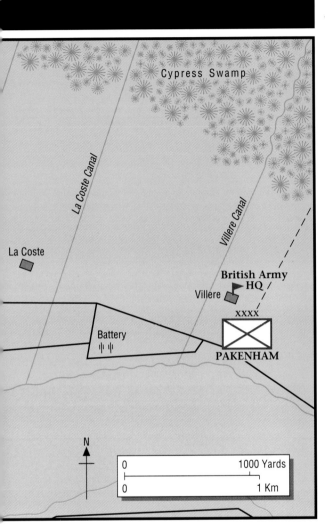

*La Coste Canal*

Cypress Swamp

*Villere Canal*

La Coste

**British Army HQ**

Villere

xxxx

Battery

**PAKENHAM**

N

| 0 | 1000 Yards |
|---|---|
| 0 | 1 Km |

◀ *The attack of 1 January depended heavily on artillery to blast openings for the attacking columns. The soft earth, lack of heavy artillery and shortage of ammunition prevented Dickson from completing the task he was given. The infantry was not ordered to attack, and this contributed to the demoralization of the troops, particularly those in General Gibbs's column.*

ning the guns back up after recoil a backbreaking task. Damage to the guns was minimal, being confined to one howitzer and a few broken wheels, but with the American guns still firing and no breach in Line Jackson, the attack was postponed.

The only unit that had advanced was Lieutenant-Colonel Rennie's. His skirmishes again pushed through the cypress swamp towards the American left to clear it of 'dirtyshirts'; they halted about noon when the artillery ceased firing, and soon received the order to withdraw. As they returned they found the body of Lieutenant Wright, RE. He had obviously been hit by a stray bullet, as he still had his weapons and telescope. 'Hunting parties' always stripped their victims of such useful items.

Considering the noise made during the night, it is surprising that Jackson, who must have been anticipating an attack, was still in his headquarters with his officers when Dickson's first cannonballs crashed through the walls, causing panic but harming no one. Perhaps they were sheltering from the rain.

The day before, General Villeré of the New Orleans Militia, whose son had been put under arrest by Jackson on the night of the 23rd and was still incarcerated, had arrived from the coast, where he had gathered 300 of his men to join Jackson's force. He and his men had been sent to cover the part of Bayou Bienvenue that emerged behind Jackson's lines, to prevent the possibility of the British surprising him there.

With every day that passed the force was becoming stronger and more confident. The initial panic of being in a house under accurate artillery fire passed as the officers ran to their positions in the line with their men. It was clearly the British intention to wipe out the American guns and make a breach in the line. The British gunners were good, and destroyed the carriages of a 12pdr, a 24pdr, and one of the big 32pdrs in Dominique You's battery, as

short supply for an all-out cannonade. The rain ceased before dawn, but a thick fog settled over the field as the two British assault columns formed. Showers cleared the fog as the morning wore on, and at 0900 the British guns started firing.

The targets were the Macarté house, thought to be a powder store, and the artillery positions. Several of the American guns did cease firing after obvious hits, and rockets blew up two caissons of ammunition. The fire continued for three hours and then ceased; as Dickson had feared, he had run out of ammunition. For the last hour British fire had been slackening. The 18pdrs with their naval carriages were even harder to manage than anticipated, and the poor state of the gun platforms made run-

well as the two artillery wagons hit by rockets, one of which contained 100 rounds. But ammunition was not a problem, and the American artillery concentrated on trying to knock out the British guns.

As the British artillery fire slackened and finally ceased, the Americans never considered the possibility that their opponents might be out of ammunition; obviously superior gunnery had damaged or destroyed them all. Jackson's men were ecstatic. Some British deserters had told Jackson of heavy guns that were to be brought up from the fleet, and of more troops that would soon be landing, but Jackson now had something he could never have dreamed of when he arrived. Not just an army, but one that, in its own mind, had been twice victorious over troops they still had to face. The British superiority in morale had vanished, and it was superior morale that had been the deciding factor at Bladensburg and Baltimore.

Jackson renewed the building work on 2 January 1815, and by the 6th the line was finished to his satisfaction. At no point was it less than 14ft deep. All the while the guns continued to fire on the British outposts. On the afternoon of the 7th Jackson went to the upper floor of the Macarté house with a telescope to observe the British lines, where noise had indicated that a lot of activity was going on. He saw

▲ *The American left wing defended by Coffee's Tennesseeans. This mid-19th-century print is surprisingly accurate in showing both the style of dress and method of fighting of the militia. Although they were more familiar with backwoods fighting, the combination of defence works and artillery gave them a steadiness against formed troops which they otherwise would have lacked. (Anne S.K. Brown Military Collection, Brown University)*

the troops 'working on pieces of wood which we concluded must be ladders'; fascines were also being assembled.

After dark there was the sound of working parties in the British artillery batteries evacuated on 1 January. Jackson visited every American battery, encouraging his men on the eve of battle. 'I do not know if the British plan to redouble their efforts or apply themselves elsewhere,' he said. 'I am preparing for either event.'

### The Final Push

Withdrawing the guns from the British advanced battery after the artillery duel of 1 January was a monumental task. The 18pdrs had to be moved before dawn on the 2nd, but constant rain added to the naturally high water table was turning the ground into a quagmire. The first party assigned to the job gave up and deserted. Pakenham was awakened, and he himself oversaw the operation with another detachment from Gibbs's brigade, men of the 21st and 44th. Strangely, although Keane's brigade had suffered most in the reconnaissance in force, it was Gibbs's brigade where morale appeared to be crumbling, significantly so in the 44th.

During the day of the 3rd a private of the US 44th Infantry deserted and made his way to Pakenham with valuable information. The Americans planned to try Dickson's trick and use hot shot against the remaining outbuildings of the Bienvenue plantation, where they assumed (rightly) the ammunition reserves were held. This information enabled the ammunition to be removed and placed in tents in the field, away from the buildings. Sure enough, on the 5th and 6th the fire came in, but the only damage was to the slave huts. The American was also able to confirm to Dickson that his cannonade had done no significant damage to the US guns.

On the afternoon of the 3rd Major General Lambert arrived at British headquarters, and 24 hours later his brigade of the 7th and 43rd followed. These superb troops, fresh off the ship, added much needed muscle to the weakened, disheartened body of the British Army. More importantly, Pakenham now had a strategy for overcoming the defences of Line Jackson. Actually, the idea had been put forward by Admiral Cochrane, who suggested that the annoying US battery on the West Bank be taken. Not only would this prevent its use against Keane's flank, but the captured guns could immediately be turned against the USS *Carolina* and Jackson's right flank. The American right could then be assaulted by Keane's column while the artillery cannonaded the rest of the line. This should encourage Jackson to support his right, weakening his left to do so. Then the main attack led by Gibbs would assault Jackson's left, and on their success would depend the success of the battle. As an added touch, part of the Rocket Troop would be sent across the river so that, after the West Bank battery was taken, they could march upstream and fire their rockets over the city to intimidate the civil government.

The key to all this was getting a British force across the river quickly enough. Admiral Cochrane

also came up with the key. The Villeré canal, by which the troops had arrived, must be lengthened until it cut the levee. Troops could then be loaded on boats in the canal and rowed out into and across the river.

Immediately, working parties of sailors and soldiers under the direction of the Royal Engineers began the task that was ordered to be completed by the night of the 6th.

## Awaiting the Blow

On the same day that Lambert's brigade arrived at the British camp, Jackson got reinforcements of his own, Major General John Thomas and his 2,368 Kentuckians. But Jackson was not pleased. Only 700 of them were armed. 'I never in my life seen a Kentuckian without a gun, a pack of cards, and a jug of whiskey,' he declared incredulously. They were also pitifully short of clothing, their march having reduced them to rags. $16,000 was raised by public subscription to purchase blankets, which were made up into coats, breeches, etc., by the ladies of New Orleans. It took only a week to make or produce a vast quantity of clothing, but as they had arrived on the 4th and the battle was fought on the 8th, some of the Kentuckians still wore the rags in which they had arrived.

At 0700 on the 7th Jackson gave his orders to the Kentuckians. Those under arms would stay with him; the rest would march back to Line Dupre, his first line of defence, and 400 would continue to the city, where they would take 400 muskets from the militia still there and then be ferried across to march to reinforce General Morgan. Since Morgan and his men had been ordered to the West Bank, he had shown no more determination than before.

Jackson's main purposes in establishing the West Bank battery were to guard against the possibility of his line being outflanked by a British vessel and to provide extra support for his right. The possibility of these guns being taken and used against him does not seem to have occurred to him until some time later. It does not seem to have occurred at all to General Morgan. He had sighted every gun to cover the field in front of Jackson's position, with no flank defence save a ditch running for 2,000 yards inland from the levee with a mud embankment thrown up

*Sergeant, 14th Light Dragoons. Illustration by Bryan Fosten.*

on the battery side. When warnings from Jackson reached him, Morgan used his troops to try to strengthen his position with a redoubt and bastion to Latour's design, but the redoubt was too small and the bastion remained uncompleted.

At 0400 in the morning on 7 January the Kentuckians arrived exhausted and mostly unarmed, as they had not found the promised muskets in the city. With supreme idiocy they had been sent forward to reinforce Major Payne Arnaud and 120 men of the 6th Louisiana Militia acting as an advance guard. On 7 January the force consisted of the Regiment of Drafted New Orleans Militia under Colonel Declouet, the 2nd Louisiana Militia under Colonel Zenon Cavallier, and the 1st Louisiana Militia under Colonel J. B. Dejan with a detachment of the 6th Louisiana: 546 men in all.

Morgan now had 1,066 men, all inexperienced and mostly poorly armed, which he divided equally between an unfortified advance post and a poorly fortified rampart and battery. If Pakenham's attack on the West Bank were to fail, it would be no fault of General Morgan.

Problems had arisen for General Pakenham. The extension of the canal would obviously not be completed by the night of the 6th, and the navy was having difficulty finding sufficient boats to carry the 1,100 men across the river. The force was to consist of the 85th, 5th West India, and a party of Marines and sailors supported by two 9pdr cannon and two howitzers. Two boats with bow chasers were to row close to the bank, protecting the flank. The expedition commander was to be Colonel Thornton of the 85th, who was instructed to send up a rocket as soon as he had taken the position, or show a blue light if he could not carry it.

The boats for the expedition were to be brought as far down the canal as possible and a dam built behind them. The canal was to be extended through the levee to the river bank, but not completely cut through. The troops would then be loaded in the boats and the bank cut. The river being higher than the canal, the water would pour in but be held back by the dam, thus raising the water level and allowing the boats to be rowed out into the river. But the ground was so soft that the excavated earth kept falling back into the canal, and extra shorings were needed as the cutting approached the river.

On the evening of 7 January, after issuing his orders for the attack on the following morning, Pakenham went to inspect the canal and the 41 boats that had been brought up from the fleet. According to Harry Smith, after inspecting the dam he turned to his engineer officer and asked: 'Are you certain that the dam will bear the weight of water that will be upon it when the banks of the river are cut?' 'Perfectly,' came the reply, followed by the qualification: 'I should be more so if a second dam was constructed.' The tone in which all this was said left Harry Smith with the impression that 'the Engineer was positive'. Although he does not actually name the officer, we can probably assume that Smith was referring to Colonel Burgoyne.

Satisfied that all plans were made, General Pakenham returned to his headquarters and went to bed. At 2100 that night, with great difficulty, the levee was cut, though not quite as deep as planned. The first boats were almost through when disaster struck. The dam collapsed, and the boats stuck in the cutting. With superhuman effort the sailors had dragged 30 boats into the river by 0315, sometimes sinking waist deep in the cloying Mississippi mud.

At 0500, when General Pakenham arose, only two more boats were in the river, and he was shocked to learn that Thornton had not yet departed. This information brought with it the realisation that, whatever happened, Thornton's attack could not assist in the main battle. Immediately he sent for information on who had embarked. The news came back that the 85th and Royal Marines, a total of 460, were on the river, and that the boats they were in would hold 100 more. Pakenham ordered a party of sailors under Captain Money, RN, to take those places, and instructed the brigade to depart at once. The artillery and 5th West India were ordered to rejoin the main army.

Once again General Pakenham was in a dilemma. His plan of attack was already going wrong, but his troops, who had twice been withdrawn from Jackson's line, were ready to attack. Every day Pakenham delayed, Jackson's line grew stronger and the foul weather took a greater toll on the British.

As dawn began to break, Pakenham was talking to Harry Smith. Low cloud and mist were almost as thick as fog over the field. If the army waited until Thornton had carried the West Bank batteries, the

*Private, Royal Marines. Illustration by Bryan Fosten.*

attack would be made in full daylight. Of course, it could be called off yet again, but there was a third course. Smith counselled delay, to which Pakenham replied: 'It is now too late'.

During the river crossing, the current had carried Thornton's brigade 1,000 yards downstream from their designated landfall. At dawn they were in the process of disembarking when they noticed a signal rocket followed by the sound of heavy artillery. The battle had begun.

# THE BATTLE OF NEW ORLEANS

### 8 January with Jackson

The American force waiting to receive the attack was formidable indeed. It consisted of about 6,700 men, of whom 4,000 manned the defence works of Line Jackson, which now had eight batteries. From the river they were:

| | |
|---|---|
| Battery 1 (the old brick kiln) | two 12pdr howitzers with a mortar at the rear |
| Battery 2 | one 24pdr |
| Battery 3 | two 24pdrs |
| Battery 4 | one 32pdr |
| Battery 5 | two 6pdrs |
| Battery 6 | one 18pdr and one 4pdr |
| Battery 7 | one 12pdr and one 4pdr |
| Battery 8 | one 9in howitzer. |

More importantly, the guns were served by expert artillerymen, many from the navy, and of course the pirates, who affected a rudimentary uniform by wearing red shirts. Dominique You had personal command of Battery No. 3.

The morning of 8 January was cold, with a heavy mist that the sun had yet to burn off, when the American line saw the British signal rocket arc skyward and burst, and heard the drums strike up. The US artillery immediately answered by opening up all along the line. For a while nothing could be seen through the mist except the muzzle flashes of the supporting British artillery.

Gradually, as the columns drew closer and the mist lifted slightly, a skirmish line of riflemen could be seen, and then two columns, one marching down

◀ *A contemporary view of the battle on 8 January, showing both columns of attack and, unlike many later illustrations, British troops on the defence works at both flanks. In the centre, General Jackson directs reinforcements to both flanks. (Courtesy of the Neal Auction Company, New Orleans)*

▲ *By far the most accurate depiction of the battle is that by the artist Laclotte. The attack on the American flanks and the oblique march of the Highlanders are clearly shown, as is the American camp and the reserves, which are usually ignored. (Courtesy of the Neal Auction Company, New Orleans)*

the levee road for the right flank and one for Battery 8, the former left flank that was almost turned on 28 December.

American artillery was firing all along the line and from the West Bank but, even with balls ripping holes in the columns, the lines were re-dressed and the troops marched on. The regulars and some of the better-disciplined militia held their fire until the British were closer, but at 200 yards the commands of Caroll and Adair opened fire without orders.

After only one initial volley, the Kentuckians loaded and fired at will, some climbing to the top of the defences to get a better shot. Suddenly the column attacking the right flank split, and with a sudden rush the head of the column took Battery 1. The troops supporting the battery fired at the British, and the 7th Infantry counterattacked; every soldier who entered the redoubt was either killed or captured.

More than half of this column, though, was marching diagonally across the front of Line Jackson, presenting both head and flank to the guns. As they did so, the bagpipes struck up 'Money-musk', but those of Scots descent in the line did not hesitate to shoot. As the British came closer, grape-shot was used – at 50 yards its effect was devastating.

Some British troops broke into the bastion protecting Battery 8, and Adair's men fell back. At this very moment the highlanders who had reached Line Jackson just stopped in their tracks to be shot like fish in a barrel, and at the other end of the line the British were retreating. Great confusion could be seen at the head of the British column in front of

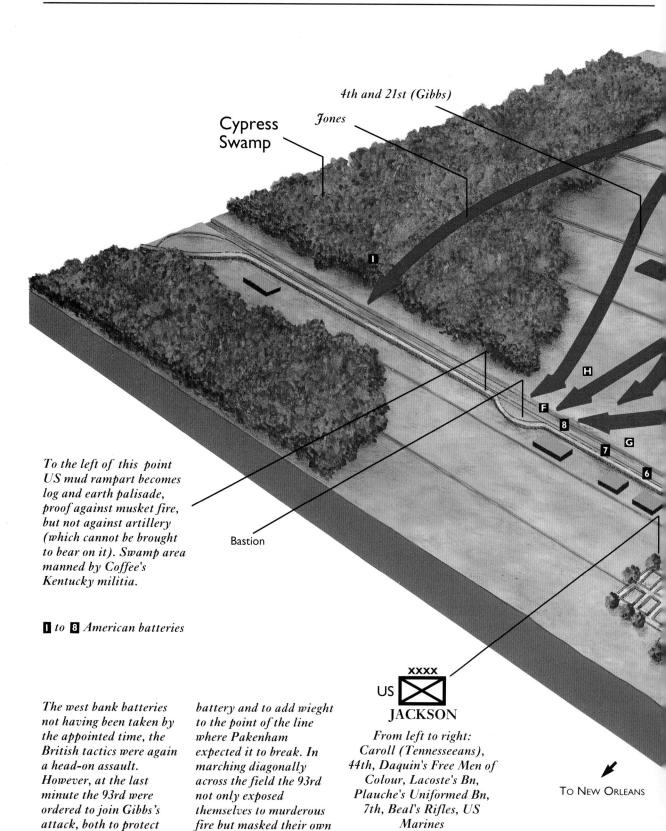

**Cypress Swamp**

*Jones*

*4th and 21st (Gibbs)*

I

H

F

8

G

7

6

To the left of this point US mud rampart becomes log and earth palisade, proof against musket fire, but not against artillery (which cannot be brought to bear on it). Swamp area manned by Coffee's Kentucky militia.

Bastion

**I** to **8** *American batteries*

The west bank batteries not having been taken by the appointed time, the British tactics were again a head-on assault. However, at the last minute the 93rd were ordered to join Gibbs's attack, both to protect them from the untaken battery and to add wieght to the point of the line where Pakenham expected it to break. In marching diagonally across the field the 93rd not only exposed themselves to murderous fire but masked their own supporting guns.

xxxx

US ⊠

**JACKSON**

*From left to right: Caroll (Tennesseeans), 44th, Daquin's Free Men of Colour, Lacoste's Bn, Plauche's Uniformed Bn, 7th, Beal's Rifles, US Marines*

↘ TO NEW ORLEANS

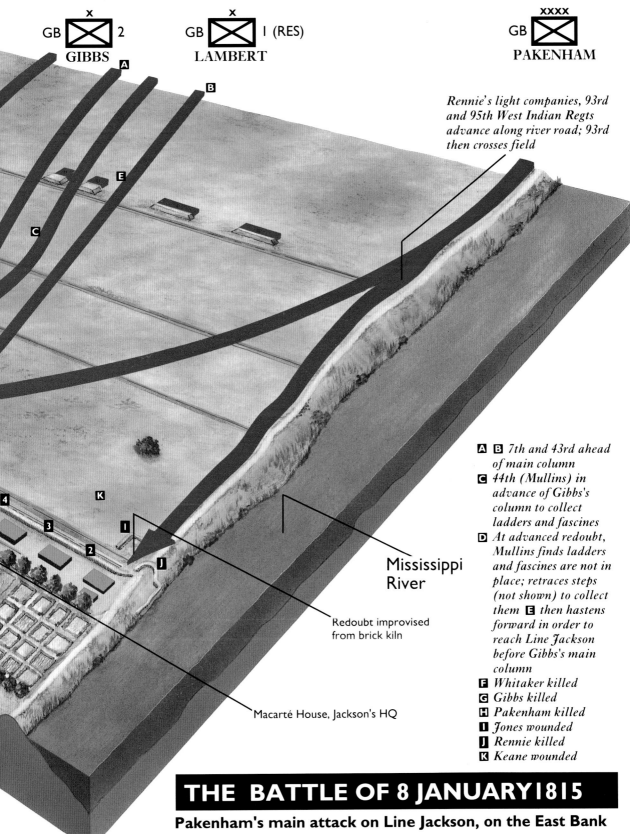

GB [x] 2
**GIBBS**

GB [x] I (RES)
**LAMBERT**

GB [xxxx]
**PAKENHAM**

*Rennie's light companies, 93rd and 95th West Indian Regts advance along river road; 93rd then crosses field*

Mississippi River

Redoubt improvised from brick kiln

Macarté House, Jackson's HQ

**A** **B** *7th and 43rd ahead of main column*
**C** *44th (Mullins) in advance of Gibbs's column to collect ladders and fascines*
**D** *At advanced redoubt, Mullins finds ladders and fascines are not in place; retraces steps (not shown) to collect them* **E** *then hastens forward in order to reach Line Jackson before Gibbs's main column*
**F** *Whitaker killed*
**G** *Gibbs killed*
**H** *Pakenham killed*
**I** *Jones wounded*
**J** *Rennie killed*
**K** *Keane wounded*

# THE BATTLE OF 8 JANUARY 1815

**Pakenham's main attack on Line Jackson, on the East Bank**

▲ *The British position between the swamp and the river, seen from Battery No.3. The small flag in the centre of the picture marks the approximate position of the Advanced Redoubt. (Author's photograph)*

▼ *The American defences from the British advanced redoubt. From left to right, the funnel of the* ship *in the slipway marks the approximate position of Jackson's headquarters; the structure in the form of an obelisk is the battlefield monument and marks the position of Battery No.3; the extreme right is where Gibbs attacked. From this position straight ahead was the line of march of Lambert and the reserves. (Author's photograph)*

Battery 8, where the Scots had just arrived. Order seemed to be breaking down. Horses were galloping to and fro, and dead or wounded officers were being carried off the field. The Americans were convinced that the British commander was dead, and vied with each other for the credit of killing him. As the Scots withdrew the Americans realised they had won.

## 8 January with Pakenham

Earlier that morning, as Pakenham was discussing his options with the staff, Colonel Dickson was

struggling to get the guns intended for Thornton's attack back into his batteries; batteries that were barely half finished and had no direct road to them over which cannon could be drawn. However, he was ready when the signal rocket went up and the American artillery fired their opening salvo. At least this time he had sufficient ammunition.

Also watching the signal rocket was Captain the Honourable Thomas Mullins, the son of Lord Ventry, holding the local rank of Lieutenant Colonel and at present in command of his regiment, the 44th Foot, which now formed the advance guard of

General Gibbs's column on the British right. The previous afternoon he had received written orders from the Commander-in-Chief, which were nothing if not specific. 'The advance guard is to carry forward with it, six long ladders with planks on them and ten small ladders as well as the fascines [300]. The officer commanding the 44th Regiment must ascertain where these requisites are, this evening, so that there will be no delay in taking them forward tomorrow to the old batteries.'

Mullins was obviously despondent and fatalistic about the job he had been given. 'It is a forlorn hope

*Sergeant, 7th US Infantry Regiment.*
*Illustration by Michael Youens.*

and the regiment must be sacrificed,' was his reaction. He made enquiries as to where the ladders and fascines were to be found, and was told the 'advanced redoubt'. Obviously thinking that he had complied with his orders, he did not go to see for himself where they were. When the columns of attack were ordered to assemble, Mullins marched the 44th straight down to their designated point of departure, the old batteries which, since they no longer contained guns and were the most advanced British structure, he presumed to be the advanced redoubt. He found it empty.

Meanwhile, the rest of the British attacking force assembled. The British centre, which would also act as the reserve, was commanded by Major General Lambert and consisted of the grenadier and battalion companies of the 7th, the 5th West India and the 43rd minus one company, accompanied by the dismounted 14th Light Dragoons.

On the extreme right, working their way through the cypress swamp, were the light companies of the 4th, 21st, 44th and 5th West India under Colonel Jones of the 4th. Major General Keane would again command the left with a special advance guard of the light company of the 7th and 93rd, with a company of the 43rd troops under the enterprising Colonel Rennie, who had almost been successful in turning Jackson's flank on the 28th when leading Gibbs's advance guard. The rest of the column consisted of the grenadier and battalion companies of the 93rd and 1st West India. On the British right, Major General Gibbs's column, consisting of the 4th and 21st, were expecting to storm directly over the defences, using the ladders provided by his advance guard, the 44th.

For half an hour Mullins vacillated and angrily denied misunderstanding his orders when a junior officer suggested the possibility. Finally, he sent 300 of his 427 men back to the 'advanced redoubt' some 500 yards behind his current position, where they found the ladders and fascines. The men doubled across the field 'as the crow flies', but once they were loaded down with their burdens they had to return via the road. As they were doing so the signal rocket was sent up.

The two wings advanced steadily with the centre/reserve following in their wake. As the columns approached the American lines, Pakenham, who was

advancing with the reserve, remarked: 'That's a terrific fire, Lambert!' He and his staff then galloped over to Keane and ordered him to send the 93rd diagonally across the field to support Gibbs. The reason for that order has been a subject of much speculation, but it was possibly because, with Thornton's task uncompleted, they would suffer fewer casualties joining an attack out of range of the West Bank batteries. Whatever the reason, when he galloped away to join Gibbs's column, he was in full hopes of finding everything in place for a successful assault.

Unfortunately the 44th party fetching the ladders arrived back at Mullins's position only minutes before the head of Gibbs's column, and were in utter confusion, with everyone in the wrong position. Even with his men in this state, Mullins had no alternative but to advance and clear the way for Gibbs. As they advanced with their loads, the

◀ *General Pakenham. His actions on the 8th have often been questioned but, though we can make educated guesses at his plan, his death on that day denies us knowledge of his true intentions.*

▼ *British artillery batteries begin firing on the American lines.*

▲ The British right wing. Gibbs leads his column forward, only to find that the ladders and fascines are not in place, and that the 44th are blocking the way for his troops. Instead of pouring into the American position, the column grinds to a halt and the attack falters. (Anne S.K. Brown Military Collection, Brown University)

▼ The British left wing. The brigade of detached light companies under Rennie break into the American redoubt on the river. Although the position was taken, no support came. Everyone who gained the position was either captured or, like Rennie, killed by the troops of Beal's rifles or the 7th US Infantry. (Anne S.K. Brown Military Collection, Brown University)

fascine party had no covering fire from the rest of the regiment. As men fell, killed and wounded, their comrades began throwing down their burdens and firing back. The ragged little volleys and independent fire were totally ineffective; aimed to fire over the earthworks, the bullets were flying over the heads of the Americans. Lieutenant Knight, commanding the fascine party, tried to keep order. He ordered the sergeants to draw their swords and run-through anyone who dropped his load. Mullins was nowhere to be seen. General Gibbs rode to the head of the column, but was unable to bring any order to the confusion he found.

The 95th were rushing Line Jackson while the assault party traded ragged volleys, and those of the 44th who had not reached the head of the column began to drop their ladders and turn tail. Major John A. Whitaker led an attack on the bastion and, despite heavy casualties, began to gain a foothold.

On the left, Colonel Rennie was also breaking into the American position. A ball carried away his calf, but he continued up and into the redoubt. A volley from Beal's riflemen felled him, but his light infantry followed him and began spiking the guns. If it had been supported, this attack might have turned the American right, but with skirling pipes the 93rd were marching off to join Gibbs's attack. Those of the assault party who did not share Rennie's fate were taken prisoner.

As Pakenham rode towards his right flank, he saw the 44th begin to break up and retreat. 'Lost for want of courage,' he remarked to one of his aides. As he passed the Highlanders he shouted: '93rd, have a little patience, and you shall soon have your revenge!'

As Colonel Dale of the 93rd reached the head of Gibbs's column with his regiment, a terrifying sight confronted him. The 44th were nowhere to be seen; the remnants of the 21st and skirmishers of the 95th were still trying to get into the bastion. General Gibbs rode into view, shouting at the top of his voice: 'Colonel Mullins, if I live till tomorrow, you shall be hanged from one of these trees!' He was then immediately shot dead. Almost as soon as the order to halt had left Colonel Dale's mouth, he too was struck dead. Colonel Andrew Creagh took command, but with nowhere to advance and no order to retreat, the Sutherland Highlanders, with perfect

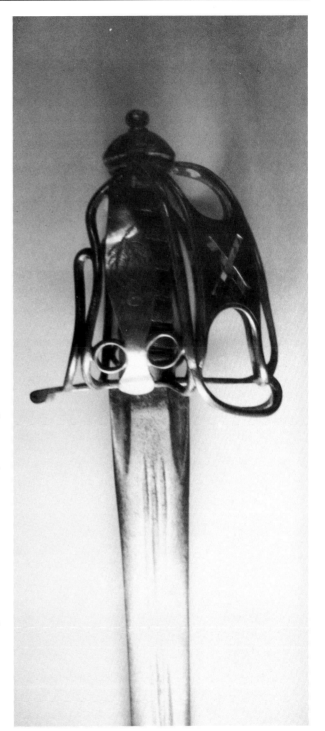

▲ The broadsword of Lieutenant H. H. Maclean of the 93rd Foot (Sutherland Highlanders). Maclean survived the battle and his daughter took this sword with her when she emigrated to America. On her death it was donated to the museum. (Courtesy of the Louisiana State Museum)

discipline and utter frustration, stood like a rock under murderous fire.

On the right, Pakenham took personal command of the attack column. As he did so he was hit by grapeshot, which shattered his left knee and killed his horse. His senior ADC, Major Duncan Macdougal, dismounted and helped the commander to his feet. Pakenham received another wound in the arm and, with difficulty, was helped on to Macdougal's horse. A moment later, as Macdougal led the horse forward, Pakenham was struck again and fell dying into the arms of his aide, ironically the same man who had found the dying Ross at Bladensburg.

Sir John Tylden, who was acting as DAAG that day (replacing Harry Smith), rode off to find General Keane and inform him that he was now in command. Instead, he found Keane being carried from the field with a bullet deep in his groin.

At about this time Major Whitaker gained the top of the American bastion, despite being wounded, and saw its defenders in retreat. He turned to encourage reinforcements to join him, but only saw British troops in full retreat. On the extreme right of the British line, the light companies of Colonel Jones had tried to turn Coffee's command in the

◀ *Top: The death of Pakenham, in a contemporary American print. In the rush to get his print to market, the engraver has put the river on the wrong side, but nonetheless gives a good impression of the two columns of attack and the central artillery position. (Courtesy of the Neal Auction Company, New Orleans)*

◀ *Below: The odd perspective of this print results from the artist encapsulating all the action into a single image, although in the engraving the scene has been reversed. The two columns of attack can be seen, and the 93rd making their march from the left to the right flank. Gibbs and Keane are both shown being wounded, while in the centre Pakenham dies in the arms of 'Major McDougall'. In this rare early version of the print Lambert stands over Pakenham making the masonic sign of distress. In subsequent editions the plate was re-engraved to show him holding a handkerchief to his eyes. (Courtesy of the Neal Auction Company, New Orleans)*

*Private, Volunteer Rifles. The Volunteer Rifle companies in Jackson's line were a sorry sight. Their clothing – which was not uniform to begin with – had become ruined by long marches. It was from these troops that the British got the idea of calling the Americans 'the Dirtyshirts'. Blanket coats were made for the troops by local ladies, but many of these were not ready until after the battle. Illustration by Michael Youens.*

▲ *A surprisingly accurate period print showing the death of Pakenham. As a shell explodes, Pakenham falls from his horse and is caught by his ADC. If, at this point in the action, there had been as many* *formed British troops in place as shown here, the position would probably have been taken. (Anne S. K. Brown Military Collection, Brown University)*

them. Lambert halted his men, ordered them to take what cover there was, and returned to the forward headquarters to confer with Admiral Cochrane. It was barely two hours since the signal rocket had set the British attack in motion.

### The Battle on the West Bank

cypress swamp. They too had failed, and were retreating with their wounded commander.

All over the field the British were retreating, mostly in disorder, and masking their own guns as they did so. The attack had fallen apart so quickly that Captain Carmichael's battery of light guns was able to fire only five rounds.

By the time General Lambert was informed that he was in command, his regiments were the only ones in any kind of order, and already American guns were beginning to cause casualties among

On the West Bank the rocket had galvanised Thornton and his force into action. They were hours behind schedule and further from their objective than intended. Morgan's first line of defence on the Mayhew plantation was outnumbered, outgunned, inexperienced, and attempting to hold a line that was too long.

As the British approached, the 6th Louisiana Militia broke. Those Kentuckians who had muskets fired three rounds before being routed back to the main defences.

Thornton, well aware of the importance of silencing the American battery in front of him, pressed on with all speed. He found an orange grove 700 yards in front of Morgan's position and reconnoitred his objective. The small redoubt by the river and three guns along the line made the American left look secure and the centre firm, but the right was so weak that it might as well have been left undefended. Thornton's plan was straightforward. Captain Money, with his 100 sailors and a company of the 85th, would feint an attack on the redoubt. Thornton, with two companies of the 85th and 100 marines, would make a direct attack on the centre, while Lieutenant Colonel Gubbins would turn the American right with the remaining two companies of the 85th. To ensure that the attack was as fast as possible it was ordered to be carried out by the bayonet alone.

*▼As the 93rd stand and are shot apart with grape, the body of General* *Pakenham is carried from the field.*

The plan worked like a charm. The Kentuckians on the right, along with a small drafted detachment of New Orleans Militia commanded by Lieutenant Colonel Philip Caldwell, broke as Gubbins and his men charged them. The Louisiana Militia in the centre, supported by the three guns, got off a couple of volleys this time, but as Gubbins swung his men on to their flank with Thornton's men charging them in front, they too fled, as did the troops in the redoubt.

Patterson's guns had been in action ever since he had seen Pakenham's signal rocket, even though for much of the time heavy mist and low cloud obscured his targets. As the British started the attack he desperately tried to bring more guns to bear on them. The victory was so swift that Patterson was even unable to oversee the spiking of his guns before he was forced to abandon them.

Thornton had captured 16 guns and the colours of the New Orleans volunteers, and taken 30 prisoners. One American was killed and three wounded. The British losses were six killed and 76 wounded,

# THE BATTLE ON THE WEST BANK

**The British offensive to capture the American batteries that threatened to enfilade the attack on the east bank**

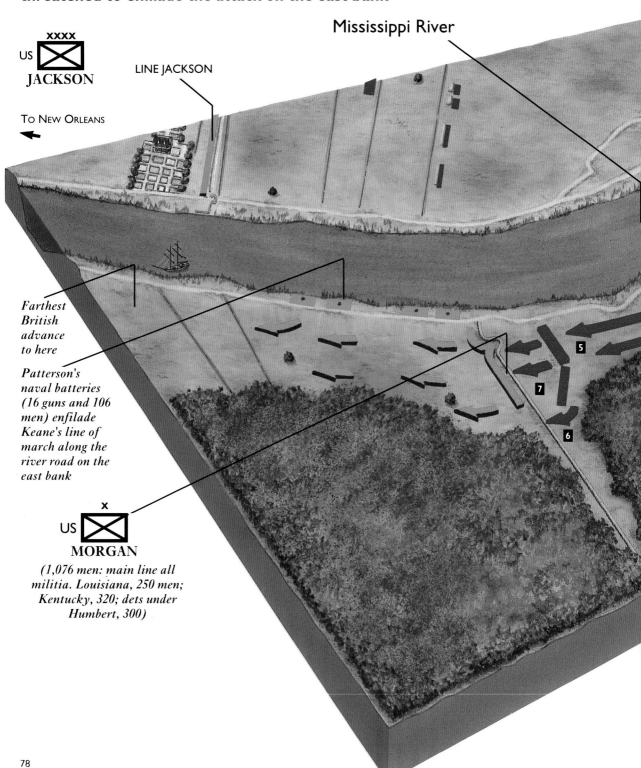

*Assembly points for Gibbs, Lambert and Keane*

Mississippi River

**US** **xxxx** ⊠ **JACKSON**

LINE JACKSON

To New Orleans

*Farthest British advance to here*

*Patterson's naval batteries (16 guns and 106 men) enfilade Keane's line of march along the river road on the east bank*

**US** **x** ⊠ **MORGAN**

*(1,076 men: main line all militia. Louisiana, 250 men; Kentucky, 320; dets under Humbert, 300)*

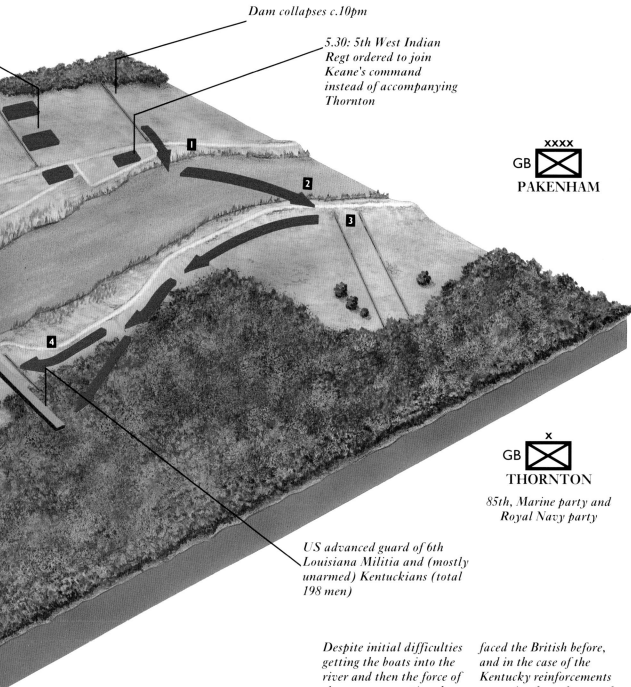

Dam collapses c.10pm

5.30: 5th West Indian
Regt ordered to join
Keane's command
instead of accompanying
Thornton

GB ⊠ PAKENHAM

GB ⊠ THORNTON

85th, Marine party and
Royal Navy party

US advanced guard of 6th
Louisiana Militia and (mostly
unarmed) Kentuckians (total
198 men)

**1** Levee cut 9 p.m. By
3.15 a.m. only 30 boats
launched; Thornton
finally departs 5 a.m.
**2** Boats taken down-
stream by current
**3** 7.30: Thornton's
brigade disembarks
and sees signal rocket

**4** c.8.30: British attack
pressed home with
bayonet for speed
**5** Thornton reconnoitres
Morgan's position c.
9.20
**6** Gubbins's flank attack
**7** c.9.55 am: Thornton
carries US position

Despite initial difficulties
getting the boats into the
river and then the force of
the current sweeping them
downstream, the attack
goes to plan – if a little
late. The urgency of
taking the American
positions is so great that
Thornton orders the
attacks with the bayonet
alone. The Americans in
this position have not
faced the British before,
and in the case of the
Kentucky reinforcements
are seriously underarmed.
Nevertheless, nothing
could demonstrate the
difference between
doubtful militia and well
trained, well lead
professionals more than
the speed with which the
American defence
collapses.

◄ *General Daniel B. Morgan, whose handling of his troops was either amazingly inept or smacked of a 'fifth column' desire for a British victory. (Courtesy of the Louisiana State Museum)*

▲ *Richard Gubbins, Captain of the 85th Foot,* *present at Bladensburg and Brevet Lieutenant Colonel commanding the regiment at New Orleans. Although Thornton had returned to the regiment and outranked Gubbins, he was being used in a superior staff position.* **(C. R. B. Barrett,** The 85th King's Light Infantry**)**

the latter including both Captain Money and Lieutenant Colonel Thornton.

As Lieutenant Colonel Gubbins, who now found himself in command, reached the American battery and looked across the river, he could see that the battle was over. He set his men to the task of spiking the American guns and pursuing the retreating foe. The pursuit had only gone some 1,200 yards when Lieutenant Colonel Harry Smith arrived with the orders issued by General Lambert after his confer-

ence with Admiral Cochrane. They were to halt, destroy the American guns, and then withdraw. The battle was over.

A short time later Colonel Dickson arrived to inspect the British position, and in looking over the artillery pieces he came across a bronze 10in howitzer inscribed 'Taken at the surrender of York Town 1781'. With this prize the troops recrossed the river and, with the rest of the army, began burying the dead and preparing to leave.

# AFTERMATH

After considering the possibility of renewing the attack, using the West Bank battery, General Lambert finally and inevitably decided on retreat. Even with fresh regiments arriving and a siege train in the hold of a ship that had just joined the fleet, the benefits of victory were just not worth the effort. British wounded who could not be transported were particularly grateful to the Ursuline Nuns who used their convent as a hospital to care for them. Other wounded, particularly officers, were cared for by local citizens. British dead were buried on the field, but heavy rain kept uncovering them and the stench was appalling. Colonel Dickson was forced to leave behind those of his guns on naval carriages; the muddy ground was so churned up that it was impossible to move them.

Several boats carrying troops back to the fleet were captured by an American cutter, which had taken the precaution of flying the Union Jack in order to approach within cannon range of its quarry. Such actions certainly helped the Americans in prisoner exchanges. Andrew Jackson, though, was magnanimous in victory. General Keane, who had dropped his sword when he was wounded, sent a message over to the American lines that he would pay any price to recover it. Jackson managed to get possession of it and sent it back with his compliments.

After sending a bomb ketch to shell Fort St Philip on the Mississippi, the fleet sailed back to Biloxi, where Lambert finally succeeded in taking Fort Bowyer on 12 February 1815. The next day the frigate HMS *Brazen* arrived with the news that a peace treaty had been signed on 24 December. Even before ratification this ended all hostilities.

▶ *'King Andrew I', a satirical print dating from the period of Jackson's presidency, when the qualities that had brought him victory at New Orleans only served to make him appear autocratic. (Marquis James,* Life of Andrew Jackson*)*

Generals Pakenham and Gibbs, who had sailed out together, were sailing back together. Their bodies had been eviscerated and packed in casks of rum, and were being sent to their final resting place in St Paul's Cathedral. Above their joint tomb is a statue depicting them in the uniforms they wore on 8 January 1815.

General Keane was recovering well, having been saved by the quality of his kersymere pantaloons. Although the bullet that entered his groin went deep, it did not break through the cloth. Instead of having a surgeon dig for it or leaving it in, the ball was removed by gently pulling the material out of the hole.

Lieutenant Colonel Dickson commanded the battering train at Waterloo in June 1815, and by the end of his career was a Major General, Knight Commander of the Bath and Knight Commander of the Guelphic Order.

The newly promoted Major Harry Smith was also at Waterloo, as Brigade Major to General Lambert, and was to go on to find fame in India. There he was Adjutant General at the battle of Maharajpur, for which he was made a Knight Commander of the Bath, later receiving the GCB for the Sutlej campaign. For his victory at Aliwal he was made a Baronet. Later he was C-in-C at the Cape of Good Hope in the Kaffir War of 1848.

George de Lacy Evans, who had been wounded at New Orleans, acted as extra ADC to Sir William Ponsonby at Waterloo. He commanded the British legion in Spain, 1835-7, and the 2nd Division in the Crimea in 1854. He became a Major General Colonel in Chief of the 21st Fusiliers, Knight Grand Cross of the Bath, Grand Officer of the Legion of Honour.

Sir John Lambert, who had been made a Knight Commander of the Bath while he was away in America, arrived on the field of Waterloo just as the battle began, after a forced march from Ostend with his brigade. He was given command of the Château of Hougoumont, the defence of which was crucial to Wellington's victory. He ended his career as a GCB and Colonel of the 10th Foot.

The battle of Waterloo was fought on the third anniversary of President Madison's declaration of war – 18 June 1815.

Vice Admiral Cochrane was promoted full Admiral in 1819 and Commander-in-Chief Portsmouth in 1821. Obviously, New Orleans had not damaged *his* reputation. Lieutenant Colonel

▼ *The Peace Medal, struck by America in 1815 to commemorate the end of the war. (Benson* Lossing's **Field Book of the War of 1812***)*

Thomas Mullins was tried by courtmartial and dismissed from the service.

For the British, engaged in the Peninsula beforehand and at Waterloo afterwards, New Orleans was just an unfortunate sideshow. For the Americans it was the turning point of their nationhood, and their one major unequivocal land victory of the war. The American forces were justly proud of their achievement, and afterwards nearly every man on Line Jackson with a musket or rifle seems to have tried to take credit for killing General Pakenham, including a member of Daquin's Free Men Of Colour. This must have been a prodigious shot indeed, as at the time Pakenham was over 500 yards away from their position and masked by the 93rd!

Unfortunately, recriminations started almost immediately afterwards. Andrew Jackson's name was omitted from the roll of honour drawn up by the city, ostensibly because of his 'high handed closure of the Legislature'. In the rest of the country, though, he was a national hero, and his popularity eventually made him seventh President of the United States. However, when he was in office, the same dictatorial attitude that had won the battle of New Orleans led some satirists to call him 'King Andrew'.

The Hartford Convention, a group of politicians from the New England states who were discussing the possibility of seceding from the union, collapsed, and the unity of the nation was preserved. Thenceforth, America ceased to look towards Europe but began to develop its 'Louisiana Territory', which at that time stretched from the Gulf of Mexico to Canada and covered about a third of the present land mass of the US, and also to evolve a distinct national character.

New Orleans went back to being New Orleans, not quite European but defiantly not American, a character that it retains to this day.

Jean Lafitte, the 'Robin Hood' figure of the battle, had his laurels fade on him very quickly. When the treasure that Commodore Patterson took from Barataria was examined, some of it was found to be the property of citizens whose ship was thought to have been lost at sea. Lafitte saw the writing on the wall and left while the going was good. For a while he and Latour were in Florida, acting as paid informers for the King of Spain. Later he lived in St Louis, where he took up his old trade as an arms dealer. His final resting place is a matter of some debate, but the author has it on good authority that it is to be found in a small cemetery 'south of the border' which is being encroached upon by the Gulf of Mexico, in a town where, even today, it does not pay to ask too many questions.

▶ *Detail from a map in* Benson Lossing's Field Book of the War of 1812 *showing the positions of the American defence lines in relation to the city of New Orleans.*

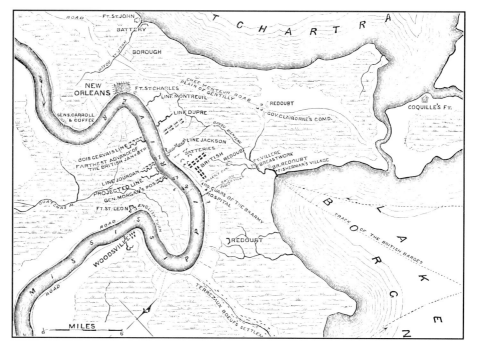

# THE BATTLEFIELD TODAY

The site of Line Jackson and the 'killing ground' of the battlefield are today part of the Jean Lafitte National Historical Park and Preserve (perhaps one day Chicago will have an Al Capone National Park). Surprisingly, there is no public transport to take you from the city to the park, but the paddle-wheeler *Creole Queen* and the tour boat *Voyageur* offer river cruises which include visits to the battlefield. The

park staff provide informative talks for the passengers, but as only a few minutes are allowed before the boats leave, they are of necessity brief.

If you wish to study the field it is far better to take a cab or drive yourself. Leaving the downtown area on North Rampart Street, which becomes St Claude Avenue ( or State Highway 46), travel for approximately six miles until you see the well-sign-

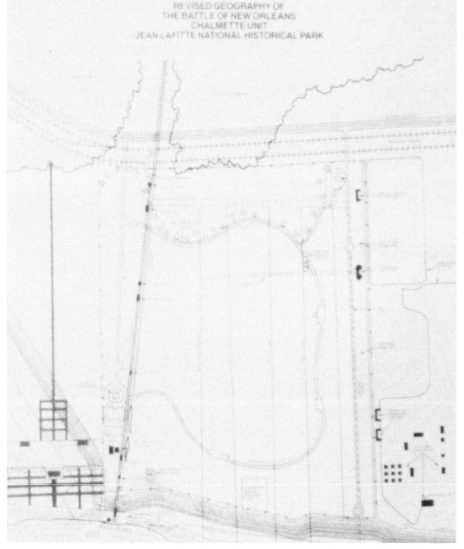

◀ *The latest map of the battlefield park, with an overlay of the features that were there in 1815. (Courtesy of the Jean Lafitte National Historical Park and Preserve)*

posted 'Chalmette National Historical Park' on your right. As soon as you make that turn, you are travelling down the American side of Line Jackson, heading towards the river. As you pass through the gates you will see on your left the reconstructed defences, and you are in the area of Battery 8, Jackson's left, which was almost turned on 28 December 1814.

The railway tracks you have just driven over mark the approximate edge of the cypress swamp of 1815.

As you drive towards the monument, which was first proposed in 1840 and completed in 1908, you will see that the gun positions have been reconstructed and give a good impression of what they must have been like on the day. You are at the posi-

▶ *The reconstructed Line Jackson at about the position of Battery No.7, showing the different construction techniques of the line in the field and that in the swamp, with the irony that the road through the American defences cuts through the line at almost the exact point that Gibbs' column was assaulting.*

▶ *The American left wing seen from the top of the battlefield monument. The field in the distance was the part of the swamp into which Jackson extended his line after 28 December. (Author's photograph)*

tion of Generals Caroll and Adair. Coffee's command extended directly behind you out of the park.

The first reconstructed Battery is No. 7, and marks the centre of the Caroll-Adair position; Nos. 5 and 6 mark its right flank. Next comes the position of the 44th Infantry, followed by Daquin's Black Militia, its right flank resting on Battery 4. Next is the position of the Free Men of Colour under Major Lacoste, and that of Major Plauche's Uniformed Militia. The last recreated gun position is No. 3, that commanded by Dominique You.

Park at the visitors' centre behind the monument, where you can see a film about the battle and a small exhibition of period weapons, including a sword bayonet of the 95th in relic condition that was excavated from the Rodriguez Canal.

Leaving the visitors' centre, turn right, and continue walking towards the river and up on to the levee. This is much higher than it was in 1815, and

▲ The line of march of General Lambert and the reserves, as seen from the battlefield monument. (Author's photograph)

◄ General Keane's line of march, as seen from the American position. The structure on the left is the present-day levee, which covers the position of the brick kiln turned redoubt. (Author's photograph)

◄ Line Jackson, looking from Battery No.3 to the swamp. (Author's photograph)

covers the position of the old brick kiln, and the river road down which General Keane's column marched to attack it. Stand with your back to the river, and to your left is the place where Beal's Rifles and the 7th Infantry (afterwards known as the Cottonbailers), who recaptured the position, were stationed. If you look to your extreme left, you will see a slipway cut into the levee just beyond the park boundary, about 600 yards from where you are standing. To the centre of this waterway is the approximate site of the Macarté plantation house that was Jackson's headquarters. To your right you will see a small plantation house. This was built in 1832, and was not there at the time of the battle.

Returning to your car at the visitors' centre, you may drive around the field on a road built for that purpose on the 150th anniversary of the battle. At various points there are places to stop, with plaques describing the action that took place there.

At the point where the road turns left away from the river you are intersecting the line of march of the 93rd as they were ordered away from Keane's column to join Gibbs's attack. Continuing to the British flag, you are approximately at the advanced redoubt where Lieutenant Colonel Mullins realised his mistake over the ladders and fascines. This is a good place to gain an impression of the American position. The field is as flat as a pancake, and the only feature is the American defence work, a frightening prospect if all those cannon were firing at you.

Directly behind you is a military cemetery, mainly containing the remains of Civil War soldiers. The far wall of the cemetery marks the farthest extent of the park towards the British position. It was here that Lambert's brigade was formed as the reserve during the battle.

Shortly after leaving this point the road turns left towards the American position and runs by a small

▶ *The Canal ditch, now much overgrown, from Battery No. 3 to the swamp. (Author's photograph)*

▶ *The Canal ditch from Battery No. 3 to the river. (Author's photograph)*

wood on your right. This is not the cypress swamp of 1815, but is maintained to screen the park from the road. You are now following the line of march of Gibbs's attacks on Jackson's left on both 28 December and 8 January. The road has a slight kink in it as it goes around a small extension in the tree line; this is where the 93rd stood in column without orders, being shot apart by musketry and grape. About 20 yards to your right, in the trees, is where General Pakenham fell. There is a move to clear this section of trees so that this very important area of the field will again look as it did in 1815.

The road continues through the American lines to join the road by which you came in. Ironically, you have passed through the very section of the defences that the British Army failed to pass over during the battle. Turning right, leave the park and continue down State Highway 46, and you will see a sign for the military cemetery on your right. Turn in here, and you will find the National Park Service headquarters on your left. The grass directly in front of this building was the position of the RHA rocket battery during the battle.

There is not really anything else to see. Leaving the cemetery, turn right again, continuing down 46 for approximately 1½ miles, and you will come upon an island between the dual carriageways, on which stand the remains of Versailles, the grandly named De La Ronde plantation house that was the British forward headquarters. On your right is Delaronde

Park, which contains the misnamed Packingham Oaks, originally the trees flanking the carriage drive from the house to the river.

As you will have seen on your travels, the rest of the sites connected with the British are under the various shipping installations or the Aluminium factory. Some of the old Villeré plantation ruins reportedly remain, but they are now on the site of a sewage farm and consequently 'off limits', apparently even to National Park employees who wanted to survey them.

Turn left as you leave Delaronde Park and, as you head back towards the city, stop to see the museum at Jackson Barracks. The road passes straight through it, so just look for the sign and turn right. Most of the exhibits relate to the Second World War and later, but they do have some earlier weapons there, and it would be a shame to miss them.

On the West Bank, Morgan's main defence line still exists, but it is part of the grounds of a school, Aurora Academy, and special permission is needed to visit it. However, it has not been maintained, and there is not much to see.

Back in the city proper, the Historic New Orleans Collection has many documents and prints relating to the battle, some of which are in a permanent exhibition. The Louisiana State Museum, housed in the renovated 'Cabildo' due to reopen in 1994, will also have a display of artifacts relating to the battle. The building itself is where the American

▶ *Gibbs's line of march with the swamp to his right, which masked his column until he was within 700 yards of the American line, from which position this view was taken. (Author's photograph)*

▶ *The ruins of the De La Ronde house. While this photograph was being taken, workmen were engaged in reducing the height of the ruins because they had been deemed unstable. (Author's photograph)*

◀ *The line of march of the 93rd, diagonally across the field from Keane's column to Gibbs's attack. The small gap in the trees in the centre of the picture is the point where the main British assault was concentrated. (Author's photograph)*

copy of the Louisiana Purchase was signed, and was the seat of the Legislature in 1815. The gardens it overlooks, Jackson Square, was the Place d'Arms where Jackson reviewed his troops when he arrived to take command. Items in the collection include the sword of Lieutenant H. H. Maclean of the 93rd, the sword of General Villeré, and a rifle marked to the 3rd Battalion 95th Foot, which was captured during the night battle on 23 December, along with uniform coats and other artifacts. Also in the city, at 941 Bourbon Street, is one of the oldest buildings in Louisiana, which is claimed to have been owned by the Lafittes as a hideout, masquerading as a blacksmith's shop. As this book was being written, a document came to light which proved that the Lafittes had indeed used the property but, more appropriately, as a butcher's.

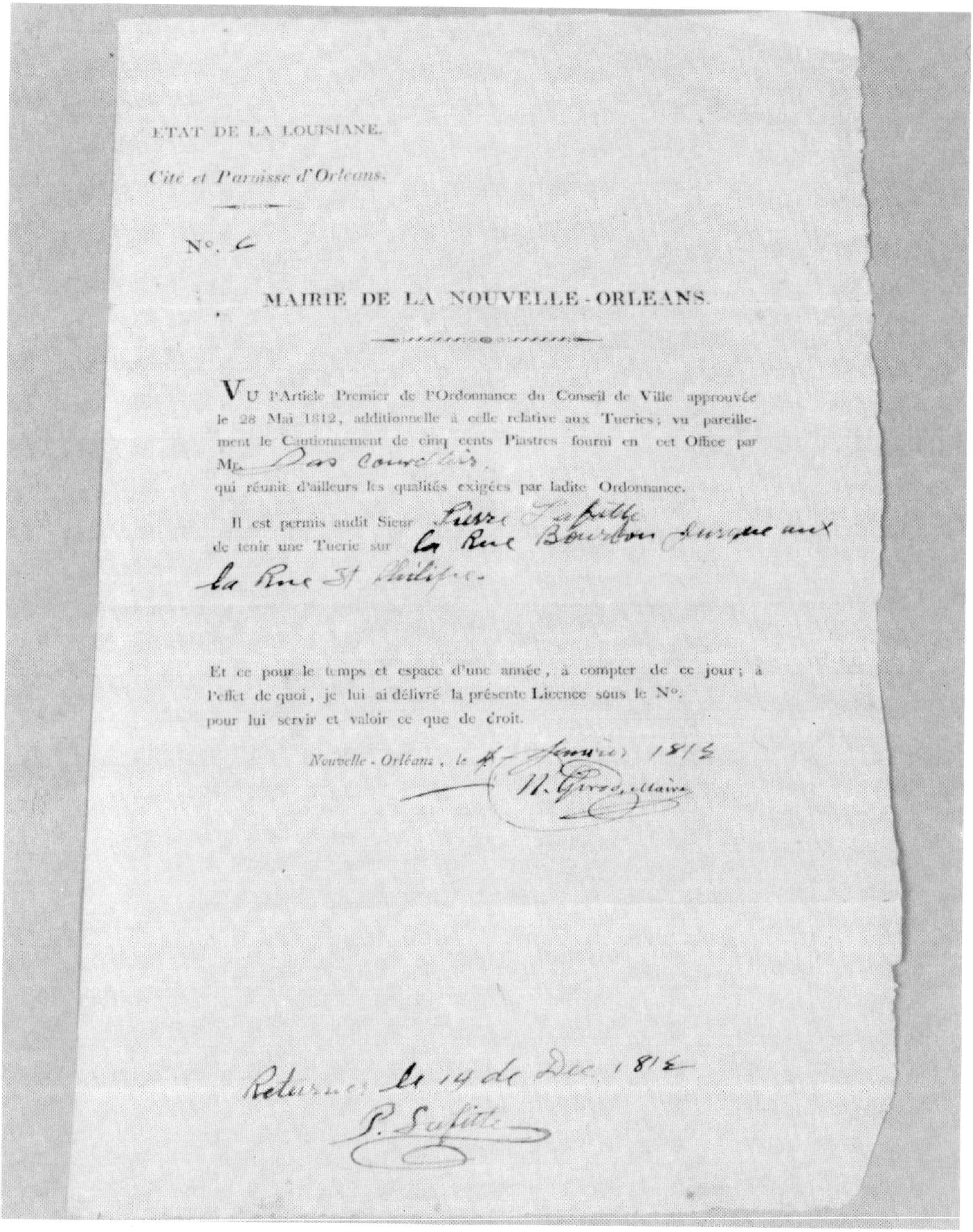

ETAT DE LA LOUISIANE.

*Cité et Paroisse d'Orléans.*

N°. *6*

## MAIRIE DE LA NOUVELLE - ORLEANS.

VU l'Article Premier de l'Ordonnance du Conseil de Ville approuvée le 28 Mai 1812, additionnelle à celle relative aux Tueries ; vu pareillement le Cautionnement de cinq cents Piastres fourni en cet Office par Mr. *Des courcelles*, qui réunit d'ailleurs les qualités exigées par ladite Ordonnance.

Il est permis audit Sieur *Pierre Lafitte* de tenir une Tuerie sur *la Rue Bourbon jusque aux la Rue St Philippe.*

Et ce pour le temps et espace d'une année, à compter de ce jour ; à l'effet de quoi, je lui ai délivré la présente Licence sous le N°. pour lui servir et valoir ce que de droit.

Nouvelle - Orléans, le *6 Janvier 1813*

*N. Girod, Maire*

*Returnes le 14 de Dec. 1813*

*P. Lafitte*

▲ *This remarkable document came to light as this book was in preparation. It is a licence from the mayor of New Orleans to Pierre Lafitte, allowing him to operate the property on Bourbon Street (very appropriately) as a butcher's shop. (Courtesy of The New Orleans Auction Company)*

# CHRONOLOGY

**1812**
**18 June** United States declares war on Great Britain
**12 July** American forces under Hull invade Canada
**17 July** Fort Michilimackinac surrenders to the British
**22 July** Battle of Salamanca, Pakenham's brigade key to Wellington's plan
**16 August** General Isaac Brock captures Fort Detroit, Hull surrenders
**13 October** Battle of Queenston Heights. General Brock killed, Americans defeated
**17-19 December** Americans destroy Miami Indian villages to quell revolt
**1813**
**27 April** Americans capture and burn York (Toronto)
**27 May** Americans capture Fort George
**29 May** British attack on Sackets harbour fails
**6 June** Americans defeated in night battle at Stony Creek
**21 June** Battle of Vittoria, French in Spain decisively beaten
**30 August** Indian massacre at Fort Mims; outbreak of Creek War, Jackson mobilizes militia on his own authority
**9 November** Jackson wins his first victory at Talladega
**11 November** Battle of Chrysler's Farm. Devastating defeat for the American army; threat to Canada eliminated
**19 December** British capture Fort Niagara
**1814**
**1 April** Napoleon abdicates for the first time
**10 April** Battle of Toulouse, end of the Peninsular/French campaign, veteran British troops freed to join the American expedition
**22 May** Andrew Jackson transfers from militia to regular army as Brigadier General with brevet rank of Major General. On the retirement of William Henry Harrison he is promoted full Major General

**25 July** Battle of Lundy's Lane
**19 August** British land in Maryland
**24 August** Battle of Bladensburg
**24-25 August** British take Washington and burn public buildings
**12 September** Battle of North Point, death of General Ross
**13 September** Bombardment of Fort McHenry, British decide defences are too strong, siege abandoned. Francis Scot Key, witnessing bombardment, writes poem that becomes US national anthem, *The Star Spangled Banner*
**7 November** Jackson seizes Pensacola
**11 November** Jackson returns to Mobile
**22 November** Jackson leaves for New Orleans
**22 November** British fleet assembles at Negril Bay, Jamaica
**26 November** British fleet sets sail for New Orleans
**14 December** Battle of Lake Bourgne
**22 December** British troops land at Villeré plantation
**22/3 December** Jackson attacks, night battle
**24 December** Treaty of Ghent signed, ending the war of 1812
**25 December** General Pakenham arrives
**28 December** Reconnaissance in force
**1815**
**1 January** Artillery duel, British attack called off
**8 January** BATTLE OF NEW ORLEANS, death of Pakenham
**6 February** British expedition leaves anchorage at New Orleans and sails for Biloxi
**10 February** British capture Fort Bowyer
**11 February** News of peace treaty reaches General Lambert at Biloxi
**14 February** Treaty arrives in Washington and is ratified by President Madison
**17 February** Madison publicly declares the war of 1812 at an end

# A GUIDE TO FURTHER READING

Regrettably little has been published on the battle in the UK, though the appropriate regimental histories touch on it (some very lightly indeed), and the general histories of the period devote a paragraph or two to the campaign. The reader must therefore turn to American publications.

For the battle in the context of the war, *The Dawn's Early Light*, by Walter Lord, New York, 1972, is a good read with very useful page notes.

*The British at the Gates*, Robin Reilly, New York and Toronto, 1974, has a detailed account of the battle and the events surrounding it, with an excellent bibliography.

*The Amphibious Campaign for West Florida and Louisiana, 1814-1815*, Wilburt Brown, University of Alabama, 1969, a doctoral thesis by a retired Major General of US Marines, has a superb bibliography and is a very clear in-depth account which obviously benefits from the author's professional experience.

*The Life of Andrew Jackson*, Marquis James, New York, 1938, is a biography by an admirer which con-tains much useful information about the possible motives for Jackson's actions, but, in dwelling on the glory, the unpalatable incidents have been removed and replaced by local legend.

*The Pictorial Fieldbook of the War of 1812*, Benson J. Lossing, New York, 1869 reprinted 1976, contains much valuable information on the war but is flawed by local legend when it comes to New Orleans; one must remember that when the book was being researched Southerners were talking to a Yankee just before the outbreak of the Civil War.

'The Journal of Colonel Dickson RA' and 'The Court Martial of Lieutenant Colonel Mullins' have both appeared in the *Louisiana Historical Quarterly*, but the former has not been published in England and the latter has not been reprinted since the first edition in 1815.

Regrettably, all the titles mentioned above are now out of print.

# WARGAMING NEW ORLEANS

Hindsight, an inevitable problem when recreating historical engagements as wargames, makes New Orleans appear unlikely (especially to British players) to produce challenging and entertaining encounters on the tabletop. Even the most patriotic American may find little pleasure in massacring leaderless redcoats in a giant 'turkey shoot' where the ultimate issue of the battle is not in doubt. Can any interesting wargames be devised, based on this Napoleonic Gallipoli?

Rather than examine again the numerous methods of wargaming Napoleonic campaigns and battles described in previous volumes in the series, this section concentrates upon the two engagements of the New Orleans campaign that appear most suitable for recreation as wargames. Since this book is devoted to an amphibious operation, it seems appropriate to present ideas for wargaming tactical engagements on water and ashore. In addition, as a change from wargames with models, there is an outline for a committee game that may prove interesting to those who have finished the account of the battle. Finally, some suggestions are offered for games the outcome of which could change the course of history.

The Naval Battle on Lake Bourgne offers an unusual subject for a naval wargame: instead of a conventional battle between warships, 42 British launches must pull hard against the current, under fire, to close with and board 5 becalmed American gunboats. The former, armed with short-range carronades and carrying sailors and Royal Marines, will have the advantage of numbers and manoeuvrability once they close with the enemy; the latter, moored with springs on their cables, can turn to bring their guns to bear but cannot manoeuvre under sail, so they must sink the launches before the British come alongside and board them. The entire action could be recreated by using 1/1200 or 1/300 scale models to represent each gunboat and launch: the British approach being gamed by adapting the gunnery and

movement systems from one of the sets of Napoleonic naval rules; boarding actions by a simple mathematical formula reflecting the numbers and morale of the opposing parties.

Alternatively, rather than attempt to portray the whole battle, the wargame could concentrate upon just one gunboat and the launches attacking it, allowing the participants to use larger scale models and more detailed rules. One player would command the American gunboat, giving orders to the crew to adjust the springs to bring the guns to bear, and controlling the complex procedure of loading and aiming the guns; several others would each command a British launch, setting the boat's course, ordering the sailors to increase or decrease the stroke, aiming the carronade, and ordering the Marines to open fire. The difficulties of early nineteenth-century gunlaying could be represented by adapting the deviation table from Rohne's 'Artillery Kriegsspiel' (a military training game translated and published by Bill Leeson in *Kriegsspiel Newsletter 19*) so that the fall of each shot could be shown on the tabletop. Where a shot hits a gunboat or launch, the damage to the vessel would be determined by dicing to discover, on an annotated deck plan, exactly where the shot struck, and casualties by throwing dice to discover whether individual figures were killed or wounded. The subsequent boarding actions would be fought on a gunboat deck plan with 15mm or 25mm figures and skirmish rules such as 'Flintlock & Ramrod' or those in Donald Featherstone's *Skirmish Wargaming* or Paddy Griffith's *Napoleonic Wargaming For Fun*.

Jackson's Night Attack of 23 December offers a hard-fought contest between British regulars, caught at a disadvantage by a surprise naval bombardment from the USS *Carolina*, and by inexperienced but enthusiastic American regulars and militiamen, in which the honours were fairly even - an ideal scenario for a wargame! In order to wargame a night action satisfactorily, the players must experience two difficulties: first, in knowing exactly where they and their men are on the battlefield; and, second, in identifying strange troops appearing out of the darkness. Captain Thomas Beal's Orleans Rifles, for example, became separated from the Tennessee Mounted Volunteers so that Colonel John Coffee reported to Jackson that they had been lost. Although they penetrated into Villeré's plantation, where many were captured by British reinforcements, half of them fought their way back to the American lines. Captain George Gleig, of the 85th Light Infantry, stated that his friend Grey was so convinced that the enemy could not have succeeded in taking up position in rear of the British outposts that he refused to let his detachment return American fire, believing the strange troops to be the 95th Rifles. Gleig also described how he was able to approach an enemy battalion and almost trick its commander into surrender by pretending to be an American officer. A conventional, face to face wargame, in which all the troops are deployed in full view on the table top, will be insufficient to create this atmosphere of tension and uncertainty. Some alternative structures for recreating night fighting are suggested below.

Andy Callan's imaginative 'Forest Fight' system allows all the troops to be deployed on the tabletop, but employs a simple mechanism so that the players do not know their relative positions. As its title suggests, it was developed originally to portray forest fighting in the French and Indian Wars.

The terrain is divided into squares, whose length represents visibility at night in the ground scale being used. Each square has a code number, and its four edges are labelled A, B, C and D. The umpire has a chart showing the true arrangement of squares – which does *not* correspond to the pattern in which they are laid out on the wargame table. When a unit leaves Square 3 by edge B, for example, the umpire checks his chart to discover it will enter Square 27 by edge D, thus disorientating the players in a way that will represent the difficulty of manoeuvring at night over ground with few landmarks. Those that do exist, the plantation houses and the canals, should be in their true positions relative to each other, though it should still be possible for troops approaching a canal to strike it anywhere

along its length. (For a more detailed explanation, see Andy Callan's own article in *The Nugget*.) A recognition test must be passed before troops can accurately identify a unit appearing within their vision, so that mistakes are possible: British troops, for example, would naturally assume units appearing to their rear are friendly for a score of 1–5 on a normal die but would realise they were hostile for a score of 6; enthusiastic but nervous New Orleans militiamen, on the other hand, might be trigger-happy and inclined to fire upon any new unit unless recognised as American on a score of 6.

In a variant of the system above, but on a larger scale, separate tables are laid out to portray the various plantation houses, the British outposts, the British camp, stretches of open ground and several lengths of canal. These do not represent particular areas, but may be used whenever opposing forces come into conflict on that kind of terrain. The players do not know the 'routes' between the tables but have to find their way as best they can - the umpire can deliberately confuse players by moving their troops to the same open ground/canal table they have visited before, when in fact they are on a different part of the field altogether, and to another table when they have actually returned to the same location! Fighting on the individual tables is controlled by the players using conventional rules for small tactical actions, such as the Brigade Game rules in 'Napoleonic Wargaming For Fun'; where very small detachments are involved, skirmish-level rules may be more appropriate.

The whole game must be run to a rigid turn sequence, so that events on different tables remain synchronized (by blowing a whistle at the end of each turn, for example). Players who have nothing to do while their troops are searching for the enemy should be suitably preoccupied trying to discern WHAT is happening on other tables, and WHERE the fighting is taking place in relation to their own units. The umpire may come round and give clues, such as, 'There is heavy firing on your right!' Looking around the hall may enable the recipient of such information to deduce which is the table representing that area. Of course, if the table concerned is an open ground or canal area, then it may not, as described above, always represent the same part of the field!

Instead of laying out numerous tables, the umpire can record each unit's manoeuvres on a detailed master map of the battlefield. The players again take the roles of detachment/battalion commanders but have small personal displays of their own units and their immediate surroundings within their limited field of vision. Units that loom up in the darkness are represented by models painted black with no uniform detail: players make their own decisions as to whether indistinctly visible troops are friendly or hostile until their true identity is revealed by their subsequent actions!

Actions are chosen from a menu of suitable options; combat and morale are adjudicated by an umpire team and reported back to the players. The personal displays can be updated by the umpires after each turn, or this can be left to the players themselves, since the displays are, ultimately, only a record of the commanders' subjective impressions of the battle. If the players can be accommodated in separate rooms, cheap, battery-powered intercoms - available from high street electrical retailers - can be used for communication with the umpires, who can use them to present graphic verbal pictures of the scene to stir the participants' imaginations and to maintain the tension of the engagement. The beauty of this system is that it can be used where both sides are played or when one is umpire-controlled, without significant alteration in umpiring techniques or hardware.

Rather than attempting to refight the entire battle, the wargame could instead concentrate upon the experience of one detachment or battalion. Obvious choices would be Captain Hallen's outpost for the British, and Colonel John Coffee's Tennessee Mounted Riflemen, or Captain Thomas Beal's Orleans Rifle Company for the Americans. Any of the game structures described above could be used, suitably adapted to provide the greatest possible atmosphere and a realistically limited perspective for the participants. One player would take the role of the detachment or battalion commander; others, if available, would portray company commanders or subalterns.

My personal preference would be to set up the game in the following way. To prevent the players realising that only one unit was being gamed, the umpire team would be introduced as rival players.

Then each player would be led into a darkened room, provided with sufficient figures to represent his own command and black-painted models to represent other troops of either side seen in the darkness, and an intercom to connect him to the umpire team. Play would proceed in real time by selecting options from a menu of tactical commands and personal actions and communicating these orders to the umpires by intercom. The latter would keep up a 'stream of consciousness' description of what the player's character could hear and see, role-playing members of the unit and using suitable 'special effects' devices such as pre-recorded volleys of musketry from sound effects records to create the aural perspective. It would be left to the player to update his figures to represent the current formation and state of his command; the umpires would adjudicate movement and combat on a master map on which the progress of the player's troops would be indicated, together with the historical manoeuvres of all other units engaged that night. 'Free Kriegsspiel' would be employed to control the action, rather than rigid rules. Provided the umpires have a reasonable knowledge of Napoleonic weapons and tactics, and had studied the engagement carefully beforehand, they should experience no difficulty in running the game satisfactorily.

A further alternative would be that, instead of playing both sides, the participants take the roles of detachment/battalion commanders on one side only, while umpires control the opposing forces in accordance with the historical events. Enemy units only appear on the table top when they come within sight of the players' troops, or when they reveal their presence by opening fire. Recognition of strange units is handled as described above.

An alternative Committee Game could be based on the 8 January Council of War. The players take the roles of the officers who had to decide whether or not to renew the attack on Jackson's position after Pakenham's death: Major General John Lambert, now commanding the British army; Colonel John Fox Burgoyne, Chief Engineer; Admiral Sir Alexander Cochrane and his 'Captain of the Fleet' (Chief of Staff), Sir Edward Codrington; Major Duncan Macdougal, Pakenham's aide de camp; Major Henry Smith, Pakenham's Assistant Adjutant General.

Each player receives a personal briefing containing biographical notes on his character, details of his experiences in the campaign and a guide as to the opinions he should express at the Council of War. Wilburt S. Brown's thesis (see *A Guide to Further Reading*) summarizes their individual positions, while the *Autobiography of Lieutenant General Sir Harry Smith* offers a participant's account of the meeting (in which the author presents himself as dominating the discussion, although junior in rank to everyone else present - suitable inspiration for the player portraying Smith, if nothing else). The umpire will judge the players' success, both in acting their assumed characters and in presenting cogent arguments. Prizes could be awarded for the best performances. The discussion should result in a decision to retreat, but if it does not, the players should be asked to draw up a detailed plan of future operations, which might itself be gamed on some other occasion.

Finally, wargaming offers the chance to investigate how the New Orleans campaign might have ended if different decisions had been made, or certain events had happened otherwise. Some obvious 'alternative history' scenarios would be:

1   a campaign game in which the British are not forced to commit themselves to the Bayou Bienvenue and the Villeré Canal but can, for example, enter Lake Pontchartrain to approach the city by a different route;

2   a tactical game in which Pakenham's reconnaissance in force on 28 December 1814 is pressed home as a full-scale attack on Line Jackson;

3   a tactical game of the Grand Assault on the morning of 8th January 1815, in which Lieutenant Colonel Thornton's attack on the west bank of the Mississippi is not delayed but strikes General Morgan's position before Pakenham launches the main attack on the left bank, and the ladders and fascines are brought up by Lieutenant Colonel Mullins and the 44th so that the storming parties can scale the American rampart successfully.

Such games can prove extremely enjoyable but their results should not be regarded as 'proving' speculation on these topics in this, or other, books on the campaign. Wargames are entertainments, not scientific experiments, which (fortunately for their participants) can never recreate the pain, terror and suffering experienced by those who followed Pakenham to the Rodriguez Canal...